D1776335

The
Essential
Guide to
Kaua'i

The
Essential
Guide to
Kaua'i

ISLAND HERITAGE

Honolulu, Hawaii

Many people assisted with this project by providing information, and it is impossible to name them all, but we would particularly like to thank the following, who were especially helpful:

Pat Bacon, Bernice Pauahi Bishop Museum; Roselle Bailey; Michaelyn Chou, Hamilton Library, University of Hawai'i; John Clark; Emily Hawkins, Department of Indo-Pacific Languages, University of Hawai'i; Angie Hewitt, *Kaua'i Magazine*; Ruth Horie, Bernice Pauahi Bishop Museum; Wendell Kam, Historic Sites Preservation Office; Koko Kaneali'i; William Kikuchi, Department of Anthropology, Kaua'i Community College; Angela Lee, Bernice Pauahi Bishop Museum; Pat Palama, Grove Farm Homestead; Joe Recca; Bob Schmitt, State Data Center; Robert Smith; Christine Valles, Office of Hawaiian Affairs; Martha Yent, Historic Sites Preservation Office.

COPYRIGHT © 1988 ISLAND HERITAGE
All Rights Reserved

Please address orders and
editorial correspondence to:

ISLAND HERITAGE PUBLISHING
A division of The Madden Corporation
99-880 Iwaena Street
Aiea, Hawaii 96701-3248

(808) 487-7299

SECOND PRINTING -1989
Printed in Hong Kong

Produced by:
THE MADDEN CORPORATION

Published by:
ISLAND HERITAGE
A Division of The Madden Corporation

Written by:
RUTH GURNANI-SMITH

Editor/Project Manager:
KELLI McCORMACK

Editorial Assistant:
LAUREEN TEIXEIRA

Art Direction/Production:
THE BAPTISTA GROUP

Page Layout/Photo Editor:
SCOTT RUTHERFORD

Cartography:
ANDREA HINES

Original Cover Artwork by:
MARK A. WAGENMAN

TABLE OF CONTENTS

INTRODUCTION

INTRODUCTION

While Honolulu and Waikīkī are names linked worldwide with images of romance in a tropical Eden, Kaua'i, the northernmost of the main islands in the Hawaiian archipelago, is not a household word. Scenes from Kaua'i are, though, more familiar than most people realize because the island is so popular as a movie location—for stories set in South America, Australia, Asia and elsewhere as well as for tropical settings of both the North and South Pacific. Known, to those who know of it, as 'the Garden Isle', Kaua'i is an out-of-the-way place, a haven for those wishing to 'get away from it all'.

KAUA'I IN PARTICULAR

Kaua'i is the oldest of the populated Hawaiian islands and, according to its oral traditions, was the first of the islands to be peopled. Legends say that the Hawaiian gods came first, from Kahiki [Tahiti], through Ni'ihau and Kaua'i then on through the archipelago. Kaua'i is also the legendary home of the Menehune, a race of tiny people that were exceptional stonemasons and prodigious builders, working only at night and completing each of their projects in a single evening. It is said that if they were struck by sunlight, they turned to stone, and a lot of boulders are billed as petrified Menehune. Other islands also have Menehune legends, but on Kaua'i, they abound. Most anthropologists believe it likely that people of small stature did inhabit these islands prior to the known Polynesian migrations, and that they have simply shrunk in the telling over many centuries. Legends of the time before the Menehune tell of another people called Mu. This correlates with other prevalent myths of a sunken Pacific continent called Mu (or Lemuria), supposedly predating the more famous Atlantis. Whoever lived on Kaua'i before the Polynesians certainly possessed tools, skill and knowledge that the

Hawaiians did not have, and their exceptional feats of ancient stonework are unique to Kaua'i.

Lying sixty-three miles north of O'ahu, across the Ka'ie'ie Channel, this 6277-square-mile [1624 sq km] island, formed by a single volcano, is almost round and about thirty-two miles in diameter, rising to a height of 5243 feet above sea level at Mount Kawaikini, near its center. This peak and the adjacent summit of Mount Wai'ale'ale (5148 feet) catch the moisture-laden prevailing northeast tradewinds and are almost constantly shrouded in cloud. Mount Wai'ale'ale is renowned as the wettest spot on Earth. The average annual rainfall is around forty feet, but precipitation in excess of fifty feet has been recorded in the nine-hundred-inch (seventy-five-foot) rain gauge—the world's largest—located at the top of the mountain. In contrast, the western side of the island gets only around a foot of rain per year. Most of the mountain rain drains into the Alaka'i Swamp, a high plateau about ten miles long and covering about thirty square miles. This almost inaccessible area also shelters a number of rare bird and plant species whose natural habitats and ecosystems have been destroyed by large-scale agricultural developments and the introduction of new species (eighty percent of Kaua'i's vegetation is non-native). This natural reservoir feeds the island's extensive system of rivers and streams; Kaua'i has five major rivers, and the only navigable river in the archipelago.

Another of Kaua'i's famous and spectacular features is the twenty-five-mile stretch of northern coastline known as Nā Pali [the cliffs]. This heavily eroded and thickly forested area is backed by the desert-like red cliffs of Waimea Canyon, on the dry side of the island.

Captain Cook's first landfall in Hawai'i was at Waimea, on Kaua'i's southwest coast, in January 1778. The Hawaiians who watched in aweful wonder from the shore had never seen large ships and interpreted what they saw as floating islands, the masts being leafless trees. These Englishmen, Hawai'i's first tourists, spent five days ashore, touring the village and environs and, through sign language, learning something of the local culture from their hosts and guides. They traded trinkets for food and the ship's artist, John Webber, drew pictures of the village and its temple [*heiau*]. They left behind the venereal diseases that would quickly decimate the Hawaiian people.

The main center of government

Hanalei Bay with familiar 'Bali Hai' in background.

was at Wailua, on Kaua'i's east coast, and the ruling *ali'i* was Ka'eokulani (also known as Ka'eo). Ka'eo's son, Kaumuali'i, was the last ruler of Kaua'i, and was never defeated by the conquering Kamehameha, though he pledged his loyalty to Kamehameha in 1810 to avoid bloodshed. His loyalty came into question when, in 1816, he allowed Russian traders to erect a fort, which flew the Russian flag, at the mouth of the Waimea River, but the adventure was short-lived. By agreement with Kamehameha, Kaumuali'i was allowed to retain sovereignty over Kaua'i and Ni'ihau until his death, but when Kamehameha I died, Kamehameha II lured Kaumuali'i to Honolulu where he was imprisoned and forced to marry Kamehameha I's widow, the formidable Ka'ahumanu who, at the same time, also married Kaumuali'i's son. Kaumuali'i died in Honolulu in 1824. Kaua'i's chiefly lines were considered very high, and marital alliances with them—believed to enhance the spouse's *mana* [spiritual power]— were eagerly sought and highly prized. Those who would be Hawai'i's monarchs today, according to the succession named to follow in the event of the death of the Kalākaua line, are of this lineage, being the colateral descendants of King Kalākaua's queen consort, Kapi'olani, directly descended from Kaumuali'i, Kaua'i's last king.

Missionaries and sugar radically changed the face and fortune of Kaua'i. Many missionary descendants became successful planters, and massive irrigation on the island's dry southern plains created vast swards of green. As elsewhere in the Islands, agricultural workers from many lands were brought to work in the cane fields. Hawai'i's first sugar plantation was founded in Kōloa in 1835, and sugar remains the mainstay of Kaua'i's economy. Pineapples are no longer commercially grown on Kaua'i, but papaya and guava are becoming increasingly important and lucrative.

Though tourism has greatly increased in recent years, Kaua'i's annual visitor count still falls short of the million mark. Many of Kaua'i's visitors are regulars, some owning vacation units on the island, and the very rural Hanalei-Hā'ena area provides hideaway homes for some of America's rich and famous as well as less lofty lodgings for an interesting breed of that society's dropouts.

The countryside of Kaua'i looks like rural America in a tropical setting, but lacks the Mainland's seasonal changes. The mushrooming condominium complexes along the island's eastern and southern coasts are in the style of southern California.

Kaua'i has virtually no manufacturing industry. This lack of development, though, makes Kaua'i the most popular of the Hawaiian islands as a ready-made movie set. The diversity of scenery on such a small island greatly reduces the costs involved in location shooting and Kaua'i frequently plays the role of locations actually situated many thousands of miles from its shores.

In the 1950s, numerous movies starred the Hanalei area, including *Pagan Love Song*, *Birds of Paradise*, and *Miss Sadie Thompson*, but Kaua'i's most famous starring roles of that decade were Lumaha'i Beach and the nearby peak of 'Bali Hai' in *South Pacific*.

The sixties brought Elvis Presley

Taro fields saturate Hanalei Valley.

to Kaua'i for *Blue Hawaii* , and John Wayne for *Donovan's Reef*.

In the seventies, *King Kong* ranged the Nā Pali Coast; and in the eighties, the Hule'ia River has provided the jungles of Vietnam in *Uncommon Valor* and those of South America in *Raiders of the Lost Ark*. The Allerton cottage at Kē'ē Beach starred as the lovers' hideaway in the made-for-television movie, *The Thornbirds*, which is set in Australia.

FORBIDDEN NI'IHAU

The island of Ni'ihau, seventeen miles to the west of Kaua'i, was purchased from Kamehameha V in 1864 by Elizabeth Sinclair for the sum of ten thousand dollars. Moving here from New Zealand, she bought the island and established a cattle ranch for her children, and the Robinson family, descendants of her daughter, still owns the island and maintains the strict protection of its native heritage, requested by Mrs Sinclair.

Virtually all the island's residents are employed on the Robinson's ranch, or in one of the family's other enterprises on Kaua'i. There is an elementary school on Ni'ihau where classes are taught in English, according to State law, though on this island Hawaiian is the language of everyday life; children in higher grades attend school on Kaua'i or on O'ahu at the Kamehameha Schools. Island residents may come and go as they please, but non-resident visitors are not allowed without prior approval from the Robinsons. There have been protests by outsiders from time to time about the rights of Ni'ihau residents, but the residents themselves seem to prefer their isolation from the modern world, and we now look to them to retrieve much of our cultural heritage.

The cardinal, an introduced species to Hawai'i.

CULTURAL BACKGROUND

Some authorities see in the legends of Menehune, particularly prevalent in the oral traditions of Kaua'i, evidence of the presence in these islands of a race of small people who were already resident when the first Polynesians arrived. There is no doubt, though, that voyaging Polynesians did arrive deliberately from the islands of Tahiti and the Marquesas around 500 AD (Anno Domini) and again around 1100. Some 'experts' claim that the name Hawai'i doesn't actually mean anything in Hawaiian; others see it as an obvious variation of the name of the legendary homeland claimed by *all* Polynesians: Hawaiki, and the term Hawai'i Nei (literally, Hawai'i here, this Hawai'i) as their way of making a clear distinction in speech between a reference to their present homeland and one to its legendary namesake.

Another interesting theory now rejected by most modern historians is that the first European to discover these islands was not the famed Captain Cook in 1778—as is generally supposed—but the Spanish navigator Gaetan, who was blown off course *en route* from the Philippines to Mexico in 1542 and

Deserted beaches on Kaua'i's North Shore.

marked these islands on his charts but, finding no gold or silver, never bothered to return. The alleged Spanish visit is dismissed as being, in any case, insignificant and without any lasting effect on the islands' culture as it was not repeated. This line of reasoning might lead us far from the truth. There are many local legends that allude to white men coming to live amongst the people of these islands in the distant past, and the first English visitors noted distinctly Caucasian features in the faces of some of the natives they encountered. The most apparent evidence in support of this hypothesis is, however, the existence in Hawai'i—but nowhere else in Polynesia—of armor-like, crested, helmet-shaped headgear and ceremonial cloaks, in the royal colors of Spain; some consider this all together unlikely to be mere coincidence. These magnificent garments were made from many thousands of tiny feathers plucked from small, predominantly black native birds, which were trapped, relieved of their few brightly colored feathers and released to produce a new supply—an early example of ecologically efficient management of natural resources.

Be that as it may, Captain Cook did arrive, and with him such sweeping change that Hawaiian culture was shaken to its very foundations. The first and perhaps the most powerful influence to take hold in the Islands was the introduction of European diseases. Hawaiians died in droves. The ambitious young Kamehameha quickly adopted and promoted the technologies of European warfare. With these, his resident English advisors, and his own intelligence

and determination, he not only unseated his cousin Kiwala'o, the hereditary ruler of his home island, Hawai'i, but also conquered the rest of the islands, which previously had been governed by a family of chiefs—Kahekili, his son Kalanikupule, his brother Ka'eokulani, and his son Kaumuali'i—to whom the 'Great' Kamehameha was also related, though himself of less exalted lineage.

Trade flourished under the guiding hand of Kamehameha, and the Islands were swept inexorably into the Western world of the nineteenth century. The old rules no longer applied. For millenia the Hawaiian people had been governed by a complex system of *kapu* or restrictions that effectively regulated everything from management of the local ecosystems, through the details of daily life, to the most intimate aspects of spiritual and religious practice. These areas were not demarcated in the world of the Hawaiians. All was one—life was life. Some of the native laws appeared meaningless and merciless to the European mind, and many laws were suspended for immigrant foreigners— men from visiting ships. The Hawaiian people saw this and worried, and wondered why the gods did not intervene.

The loudest death knell for the Hawaiian way of life was rung inadvertently by the powerful Ka'ahumanu, a widow of Kamehameha. At his death he had named her *kuhina nui* [chief advisor] and set her up as co-regent with his son and heir, Liholiho. Ka'ahumanu abolished the law prohibiting men and women from dining together, which she found both inconvenient and incompatible with her esteemed position, by persuading Liholiho—Kamehameha II—to sit down and eat with her and his mother, Keopuolani, at a public banquet—an act which produced no response from the gods. She had not realized that the whole *kapu* system would thus come crashing down around the heads of her people, and she had nothing to offer in its place. Their world was shattered—their gods had abandoned them—and the Hawaiians were dazed and spiritually adrift when the first missionaries arrived from New England in 1820.

The Hawaiians had already torn down many of their own temples and chased their priests into hiding. These new invaders met no resistance from the local religion, for there was none. It was the traders and other white residents of the Islands who howled loudly in protest, over moralistic meddling.

As the newcomers acquired more land, as their trading and planting ventures flourished and grew, and as the native population continued to decline, cheap agricultural labor was brought to the islands, first from China then from Japan, Europe, the Philippines and elsewhere. Thus began the famed Hawaiian 'melting pot'. In Hawai'i today, there is no ethnic majority; this is probably the only place in the world where *everyone* belongs to a minority group. All these people naturally brought with them the languages and customs of their native lands, and with them have enriched the cultural life of Hawai'i.

As a result of the powerful influence of the missionary establishment, exercised through members of the ruling [*ali'i*] class of Hawaiians (particularly a few powerful women), and of the 'guidance' of foreign 'advisors' to Hawaiian kings, the Hawaiians— not at all grasping the full implications of Western concepts such as property and ownership—signed away their 'rights' and virtually gave their homeland to the newcomers. These rulers of the local economy—mostly Americans and many missionary-descended— eventually wrested the government as well from the Hawaiian royal line, with the help of representatives of the US government, and set themselves up as the new government of a 'Republic of Hawai'i' until they were able to persuade the US Congress to annex them outright—after which they continued to lobby for statehood. None of these sweeping decisions had much to do with the actual preferences of the Hawaiian people who were, by now, a minority.

This exceedingly brief account of Hawaiian history leaves out, of course, details and differing viewpoints of the diverse interest groups involved. Nonetheless, the result is the same.

Hawai'i was granted statehood and admitted as a fully fledged member of the United States of America in 1959, and is now squarely in the mainstream of modern American life. Its capital, Honolulu, is a thriving business and academic center—the gateway for commerce and cultural exchange with Asia, Australia and the South Pacific.

Throughout the islands which can be visited, all the modern conveniences of contemporary American life are readily available—yet it is still possible to 'get away from it all'. Hawai'i as a resort has something for almost everyone.

GEOGRAPHY

The Hawaiian archipelago spans 1523 miles [2451km] and includes 132 islands, reefs and shoals strewn across the Tropic of Cancer—from Kure Atoll in the northwest to underwater seamounts off the coast of the island of Hawai'i in the southeast. All are included in the state of Hawai'i except the Midway Islands, which are administered by the US Navy.

This southernmost of the United States lies between latitudes 28° 15' and 18° 54'N and between longitudes 179° 25' and 154° 40'W, reaching almost as far west as Alaska's Aleutian Islands.

Hawai'i's major islands share their tropical latitudes with such urban centers as Mexico City, Havana, Mecca, Calcutta, Hanoi and Hong Kong. The 158th meridian west, which passes through O'ahu's Pearl Harbor, also crosses Point Barrow on Alaska's north coast, Atiu Island in the South Pacific's Cook Islands and Cape Colbeck near the edge of Antarctica's Ross Ice Shelf. Though the name *Hawai'i* evokes in the minds of most people images of a tropical paradise in an idealized 'South Pacific', Hawai'i is, in fact, an island group in the North Pacific, uniquely isolated at about a

Kaua'i's etched Nā Pali Coast.

thousand miles from its nearest neighbors—the Line Islands to the south and the Marshall Islands to the southwest. Nothing but open ocean lies between Hawai'i and southern California, 2390 miles [3846km] to the east-northeast; Japan, 3850 miles [6196km] to the west-northwest; and Alaska, 2600 miles [4184km] to the north. The Marquesas—from which at least some of the early Polynesian migrants came—are 2400 miles [3862km] to the south-southeast.

Though Hawai'i's land surface adds up to only 6425 square miles [16,642 sq km] (at that still larger than Connecticut, Delaware or Rhode Island), the archipelago, including its territorial waters, covers a total of about 654,500 square miles [1,695,155 sq km]—an area considerably bigger than Alaska and more than twice the size of Texas.

There are eight main islands in the Hawaiian chain, one of which—Kaho'olawe—is not inhabited because it is used by the military for target practice. The tiny island of Ni'ihau is privately owned and can be visited by non-residents only at the invitation of its owners—an honor rarely bestowed on anyone. This island—due to its fierce protection from outside influence—is the last stronghold of Hawaiian culture (its entire population [226] is of at least part-Hawaiian blood), and it is the only place on the planet

Sun streams through Waimea Canyon.

where Hawaiian is still spoken as the mother tongue. Scenic helicopter flights over the island may touch down for up to twenty minutes, but no contact with the residents is permitted. That leaves visitors to Hawaiʻi the islands of Kauaʻi, Oʻahu, Molokaʻi, Lānaʻi, Maui, and Hawaiʻi (familiarly known as 'the Big Island')—in that order, north to south and chronologically in age—to play with.

Twilight glow over Waimea.

CLIMATE AND WEATHER

The climate in Hawai'i is pleasant and equable—that is, it doesn't change much throughout the year—at sea level. The temperature ranges between a daytime high near 90° F [around 30° C] in 'summer' and a nighttime low near 60° F [around 18° C] in 'winter'. There really are no distinct seasons as such. Even in 'winter' the daytime temperature is usually in the 80s. The comfort factor that this involves depends on what you're used to: where you've come from and how long you've been here. People do acclimatize. Those of us who live here start to shiver and bundle up when the mercury plummets to 75° F [24° C]. The coldest months are February and March and the hottest August and September.

Despite this lack of strong seasonal variation, Hawai'i is home to an extraordinary diversity of microclimates—from desert to rainforest. Temperature drops about 3° F for every thousand feet of increased altitude, a factor which produces seasonal snow on the upper slopes of the Big Island's Mauna Kea. Rainfall varies dramatically in different parts of each island—from a mere ten inches annually in some leeward areas to more than forty feet at the summit of Kaua'i's Mount Wai'ale'ale (the wettest spot on Earth), where it virtually never stops raining. The State's heaviest rains are brought by storms and fall between October and April. A lot of rain is needed to water all this lush tropical foliage, and drought in some areas of the islands is not unheard-of. Fortunately, most of our local rainshowers are short if heavy. There are, of course, occasions when it rains all day, but these are rare, except in the upper reaches of valleys where the rainclouds never leave for long. The windward areas get far more rain than their leeward counterparts.

There have been few damaging storms or tsunami (seismic sea waves) in Hawai'i. If you would like information about Civil Defense Warnings and procedures, refer to the front section of the White Pages of the local telephone directory.

TIME AND DAYLIGHT

The length of daylight in Hawai'i doesn't vary greatly from one time of year to the next—only around three or four hours—because of the Islands' tropical position. Thus, Hawaiians have never felt any need to save it and Hawaiian Standard Time is in effect year-round. The time differences between Hawai'i and places that do save daylight varies by an hour when daylight saving is in effect elsewhere.

Hawaiian Standard Time is five hours behind New York, four hours behind Chicago, three hours behind Denver and two hours behind San Francisco; it is also eleven hours behind London, nineteen hours behind Tokyo, twenty hours behind Sydney, and twenty-two hours behind Auckland and Suva. Add an hour to all these for daylight time.

The popular local phrase 'Hawaiian time' simply means 'late'.

INTRODUCTION

14

THE FLAG

The Hawaiian State Flag has served Kingdom, Republic and State and was designed prior to 1816 for King Kamehameha I. Most first-time visitors to Hawaiʻi are intrigued to note the British Union Jack in the corner. The Union Jack honors Hawaiʻi's early ties with Britain; the eight horizontal stripes represent the archipelago's eight main islands. Hawaiʻi's State Anthem, 'Hawaiʻi Ponoʻī', is its former national anthem and was composed by King Kalākaua.

LANGUAGE

English became the common language of Hawaiian commerce very early in the era of immigration and economic investment by Americans and other foreigners. And so it remained. The missionaries made sweeping and now irreversible changes in the Hawaiian language when they hurriedly transliterated and transcribed it for print in order to produce bibles. Subsequent efforts to stamp out the native tongue were very successful. There are only a few hundred native speakers left—most either very old or from the private island of Niʻihau, but a strong grassroots movement to save the language has taken hold in recent years and is gaining widespread support. Virtually everyone in the Islands today speaks the American variety of English, with a few local variations on the theme. Some of these should be noted because they are so common.

Perhaps most important is the local way of giving directions. The cardinal points of the compass on an island are far less relevant than the obvious 'toward the mountain' and 'toward the sea'. A contracted form of the Hawaiian words for these directions is universally used in Hawaiʻi. 'Toward the upland [*uka*]' is *mauka*; 'toward the sea [*kai*]' is *makai*. For the other directions, major landmarks are used. It makes perfect sense. This usage is nowhere near as universal on Kaua'i as on O'ahu.

Some people also have difficulty with Hawaiian placenames and streetnames. The Hawaiian language is beautiful and only *looks* intimidating to non-Polynesians because they are not accustomed to seeing so many vowels in a row. **Basically, if you just pronounce all the letters one by one, you'll be fine.** In fact you might, at that, be pronouncing Hawaiian more correctly than a lot of people who are used to it. The 'glottal stop' (written ') is the hard sound created by stopping between vowel sounds, like the English 'oh-oh', rather than a sliding from one vowel to the next, as is usual. In Hawaiian, this is called *'okina*. Just stop talking then start again immediately. The macron (written as a - over a vowel), called *kahakō* in Hawaiian, simply means that vowel is held a little longer—as if it were written twice, which it occasionally is. Consonants are pronounced the same as in English except that *w*

sounds like *v* when it immediately precedes a final single vowel and occasionally at other times. Vowels are pronounced as in Spanish or Italian (*ah, eh, ee, oh, oo*). The vowel combinations *ai, ae, ao, au, ei, eu, oi* and *ou* are stressed on the first member and basically sounded as single units, though the second vowel in the set is truly pronounced and not lost in the combination as with English diphthongs. Otherwise, stress (accent) is almost always on the next-to-last syllable. No matter how many times you hear it along the tourist trail, the very special and wonderfully soft Hawaiian word *aloha* is NOT correctly pronounced with the stress on the last syllable.

You will often see Hawaiian words written without the *kahakō* and *'okina*. This was the custom of the English-speaking people who first transcribed the language and was common practice until fairly recently. The markings are necessary for correct pronunciation of many words, and for discerning

Glory bush and vriesea flowers.

between similarly spelt words with quite different meanings. Government policy is now to insert the correct markings in all Hawaiian words on street and road signs as they are replaced. At the moment, you may see them either way.

The other feature of local language that visitors are bound to encounter is our own brand of pidgin English. It is spiced with words from the rich linguistic heritage brought by people of many lands, but basically, it is English with a bit of Hawaiian, and if you listen carefully, you'll catch on. The idiom and the lilt are peculiar to Hawai'i, but the pronunciation of most words is recognizable. Lists of commonly used Hawaiian and pidgin English words, with their meanings and pronunciations, are at the back of this book.

IN TRANSIT

GETTING HERE

A trip to Kauaʻi usually starts as a fantasy. Happily, transforming that into reality has become very easy and not all that expensive. This section discusses the several practical considerations involved in making your dream come true, and offers options you may wish to consider. Because of the vast difference in time and expense involved, most people choose air travel over sea travel, but the latter is still available; details are discussed below under Bookings. When to come is anytime, depending on your own schedule and preferences. The largest crowds usually gather in February and August.

CHOOSING LOCATION

The first order of business in planning your stay is to choose your preferred location. Most of Kauaʻi's vacation developments are clustered around the island's eastern and southeastern shores, with another concentration in the middle of the northern shore. There are small local communities along the southern shore, and a couple of small military reserves on the western shore. The rest of the island—most of its upland—is undeveloped, including 88,000 acres of forest reserves and State and County parks where some camping is permitted.

SELECTING LODGING

Kauaʻi has both glamorous suites and idyllic rural retreats, rooms ranging from upscale luxury to rustic camping with lots of offerings in between. While the island boasts several excellent hotels, most of its resort accommodations are condominiums. Many visitors—especially

Poʻipū Beach, sunset.

those traveling with children— prefer these self-contained apartment facilities. This option is usually less expensive and offers more privacy and independence. Hotels are the favorite of those who wish to be pampered during their holiday. Most of our hotels are staffed by friendly, efficient people, and most are near where the action is. Private vacation home rentals are also plentiful, and bed-and- breakfast homes and campsites are available in limited supply. Bed-and-breakfast accommodation in private homes is an increasingly popular option for budget-minded travelers and for those wishing to avoid crowds, and exclusive use of private homes is available for longer-term visits. Specific places that offer these various types of lodging are described in detail under ACCOMMODATION.

WHAT TO BRING

The usual attire on Kaua'i is casual, and apparel known elsewhere as 'summer clothing' is worn all year in this land of perpetual spring and summer. Shorts are acceptable almost anywhere, though most businesses require customers to wear shoes (rubber thongs will usually suffice). Comfortable walking shoes are a must. Sleeveless or short-sleeved shirts are usually best for day wear, but long sleeves—or even a jacket or sweater—may be needed for cool winter evenings and air-conditioned buildings. Deluxe restaurants have a dress code requiring men to wear jackets, though usually not ties.

PERMITS AND LICENSES

Licenses or permits are required for some activities in which visitors may choose to participate. The most obvious and common is driving. Any visitor who drives in Hawai'i must have a valid license from another state or a Canadian province or a current international driver's license issued in another country.

Camping permits are required for public parks that allow camping. All hunting requires a license, as does freshwater fishing; none is required for recreational ocean fishing. Further details of these sporting licenses are discussed in the SPORTS section.

Those wishing to indulge in the romance of tropical nuptials also need a license—which can be obtained from one of many marriage license agents licensed by the Kaua'i County Board of Health (PO Box 671, Lihu'e 96766 245-4495 M-F 8am-4pm). Licenses are issued immediately after application, usually within twenty minutes, and expire after thirty days. They are only valid in Hawai'i, and the nominal fee is payable in cash at the time of filing.

Numerous local companies specialize in wedding services, including renewal of vows; these services and popular wedding venues are described under Other Services in ET CETERA.

No vaccinations or innoculations are required for entry into Hawai'i.

BOOKINGS

To book your air or cruise tickets, your lodging, and any tours you may wish to arrange in advance, we recommend using a travel agent. You could spend days chasing specifics and comparing prices but travel agents have the information at their fingertips and they know their sources well. It costs you no more as the agents commission is paid by the provider, not the customer; and in many cases the agent can offer you a better deal than you could get if you booked directly. Many airlines and hotels also give priority to bookings made through agents as they are generally less likely to be canceled.

There are a couple of catch-all activity planners on Kaua'i that will book for you everything—from accommodations and car rental to lu'au, cruises/tours or even exotic weddings. **Aloha Destinations** (742-9773, 800 367-8047 x247) in Kōloa and **Paradise Hawaiian Tours & Activities** (822-0600, 800 222-7756) in Kapa'a offer these services and, by buying from the operators in bulk, can offer cheaper prices than you can get by buying directly. The **Visitor Activities & Information Center**, located in Kukui Grove Center (245-1993) and Kiahuna Village (742-1223) also handles a diversity of bookings.

Airlines

Our island state is such a popular destination that, though it is accessible only by air or sea, airfares are kept low through volume and competition. There are many airlines serving the Hawaiian Islands, most landing at Honolulu International Airport. Flight times are roughly five hours from California, nine hours from Chicago, eleven hours from New York, eight hours from Tokyo and nine and a half hours from Sydney. Domestic carriers providing service to and from the US mainland are **Air America, American Airlines, Continental,**

Delta, Hawaiian Airlines, Northwest Airlines, TWA and **United Airlines.** United Airlines also provides direct service from the US mainland to Kaua'i's Līhu'e Airport. Foreign carriers currently serving Honolulu are **Air New Zealand, Air Tungaru, Canadian Airlines International, China Airlines, Japan Air Lines, Korean Air, Philippine Airlines, Qantas, Singapore Airlines** and **Ward Air.** Please note that these lists are subject to change without notice. Your travel agent will have all the latest details and schedules.

Cruise lines

Arriving in the Islands by cruise ship is not easy these days, least of all to Kaua'i. Most of the cruise lines that make stops at our islands—**P & O Lines, Princess Cruises, Royal Viking Line, Cunard Line** and other European-based cruise operators—are of

foreign registry and are forbidden by US law from transporting American citizens from one US port to another US port. This law—the Jones Act—was passed in 1896. Thus, if you board a foreign vessel in New York or California, you may visit Hawai'i, but cannot make it or any other US port your final destination. You may, if you board ship in another country, make Hawai'i or another American port your final destination, but most cruise operators today don't encourage one-way traffic. Still, it is possible, and there really is no more beautiful way to arrive here than by sea. **American Hawaii Cruises** has two ships, the SS *Constitution* and SS *Independence*, that cruise the Hawaiian island chain on a weekly basis. They make a few trips a year to the ports of Seattle, San Francisco and Los Angeles.

If your determined dream is to come here by ship, your travel agent will be able to provide dates of upcoming trans-Pacific voyages by these US-registered vessels, or contact American Hawaii Cruises. For details of interisland cruises, see GETTING AROUND.

Harvesting taro, a Hawaiian staple, in Hanalei.

Sightseeing tours

There are not many tour companies on Kaua'i, but your travel agent will be able to book tours for you through the larger companies, if you want your trip precisely planned, or you may use one of the activity planners mentioned above. Many visitors, though, prefer to book tours after arrival and a bit of scouting around; and many of the best tours are offered by small operators not linked by telex to Mainland or foreign cities. There is no danger of not being able to get onto a tour to where you want to go so we have chosen to describe a selection of tours and tour companies under GETTING AROUND.

HONOLULU INTERNATIONAL AIRPORT

This is one of the busiest airports in the world, serving as gateway between East and West. Passengers arriving from the US mainland or from other countries emerge from the catacombs of this vast complex on the ground level of the main terminal building. The airport's second level services Mainland and overseas departures and includes ticket counters for reservations and check-in, monitors with departure information, and all departure gates.

Most arriving and departing interisland flights service passengers from the interisland terminal, located next to the main terminal building at the westward end.

KAUA'I AIRPORTS

Līhu'e has a lovely new airport with all the usual amenities, like book and souvenir shops, bar, snack shop and visitor information desks, but even this enlarged facility is not really big enough to get lost in. There are no customs and immigration facilities as passengers arriving from other countries must be cleared in Honolulu before continuing their journey to Kaua'i. Ten car rental agencies are conveniently located directly across from the arrival portals of the airport. Shuttle buses and taxis providing transportation to hotels wait in this area.

Princeville Airport is a small, private strip receiving only the flights of Princeville Airways. The terminal has a cafe lounge and free parking; the adjacent headquarters of Papillon Helicopters has a gift shop.

Transportation

Līhu'e Airport is about two miles from town, nineteen miles from Po'ipū, twelve miles from Kapa'a and thirty-five miles from Hanalei. Princeville Airport is about two miles from Princeville, three miles from Hanalei and six miles from Hā'ena.

BUS

Kaua'i has no public transportation system. Two private companies run shuttle service from Līhu'e Airport to hotels in the southeastern sector of the island. **Shoppe Hoppers** (332-7272) transports visitors and their luggage as far as Kapa'a on the East Shore and Po'ipū on the South Shore. **South Shore Shuttle** (335-6192) goes only to the Kōloa-Po'ipū area. Both have courtesy phones at the visitor information booths in the baggage claim area.

TAXI

Thirteen different taxi companies provide service from Līhu'e Airport. There are usually lines of taxis waiting outside the baggage claim area. The metered cost of a journey is one dollar and sixty cents per mile, so this can be an expensive way to travel if you have far to go. There is an extra charge for each piece of luggage. Only **North Shore Taxi** (826-6189) services Princeville Airport.

RENTAL CAR

At Līhu'e, ten car rental agencies have service desks facing the baggage claim areas opposite the main terminal building and offices near the airport. Only Hertz has vehicles on the premises; the others transfer customers from the

terminal to the pick-up point, all of which are nearby. Honolulu, Thrifty and Tropical do not have airport offices, but have courtesy phones at the visitor information booths beside the baggage claim areas and will pick up customers at the airport. For additional information on car rentals, see GETTING AROUND.

At Princeville, rental cars are available only through Avis and Hertz, both of which have offices and vehicles on the premises.

LIMOUSINE

Special arrangements to be met at the Airport by a limousine service are possible through two companies, **Limo Limo Limousine Service** (822-0393) and **Kauai Island Tours** (245-4777).

HELICOPTER

Transfers are available between Līhu'e Airport and Princeville Airport from **Papillon Helicopters** (826-6591) by special arrangement. There are no regularly scheduled transfer flights.

An overcast afternoon at Brennecke's.

GETTING AROUND

A single main highway runs near the coastline around most of Kaua'i, cutting inland across the southeastern tip of the island and stopping altogether at Polihale on the west coast and Hā'ena on the north coast. The southern portion is called Kaumuali'i and the western and northern section, Kūhiō. Between these ends of the road is the dramatic twenty-five-mile stretch of Nā Pali coastline. There are not many options for getting around, and as there is no public transportation system and taxi fares can run high, most visitors rent cars. Tours are available on land, by sea, or in the air, and bicycling and hiking are very popular on this island.

TOURS AND RENTALS

The guided tours you can take are numerous and varied. There are dozens of companies listed under Tours in the Kaua'i Yellow Pages. Exploring on your own in a rented vehicle is the other option.

Air tours

Scenic flights over Kaua'i are almost indispensable. Much of the island's spectacular natural scenery is otherwise inaccessible except by arduous and sometimes dangerous hiking and mountain climbing, and some of it not at all. The bird's eye view is magnificent. Do this first and the rest of your sightseeing on Kaua'i will be greatly enriched.

Fixed-wing overflights are available only from other islands as part of multi-island packages. On Kaua'i, it's helicopters, ideal for getting into the nooks and crannies of this rugged terrain. So popular has this sightseeing sensation become that there are no fewer than eighteen helicopter tour companies operating on Kaua'i and many residents jokingly tell visitors that Kaua'i's 'Island Bird' is the 'whirly-bird'.

The largest is Princeville's **Papillon Helicopters** (826-6591), operating with six choppers and able to accommodate large groups. Their unique wilderness landings and drop offs allow passengers an isolated natural experience of the island. Around-the-island tours are run out of their Princeville, Līhu'e and Hanapēpē offices. The best helicopter tour available is that run by **Jack Harter Helicopters** (245-3774) in Līhu'e. Even the other companies readily concede this. All flights are piloted by Harter himself, who has been doing this for more than twenty years. His flights take an hour and a half and are enriched by his deep love for and thorough knowledge of the island. There is, however, only one Jack Harter, and he runs only three flights per day—fewer, or none, if the weather is uncooperative—Monday through Friday. These are booked well ahead, so it is advisable to make advance reservations. To those unhappy would-be customers who cannot be accommodated, Harter's staff recommends **Will Squyres Helicopter Service** (245-7541). Squyres also takes all flights up himself and has been piloting helicopters for almost as long as Harter. His six daily hour-long tours reveal his broad knowledge of Kaua'i as well as his love of helicopters.

If neither of these is available at a time to fit your schedule, choose a company where the owner is the pilot and has an air taxi license (not all have this, and getting it requires more rigorous testing than a simple operator's license). Also choose a flight that spends at least an hour in the air; anything quicker will have the scenery whizzing past so fast that you'll hardly glimpse a feature of the landscape before it's gone.

Kenai Helicopters (245-8591) and **South Sea Helicopters** (245-7781) both operate out of Līhu'e Airport and offer circle-island tours at competitive rates. Kenai also provides transportation to and from major hotels.

Water tours

The next most exciting and nearly indispensable excursion on Kaua'i is a boat trip down the Nā Pali Coast. It doesn't matter if you've already seen the scene from the air; this is an entirely different perspective—the functional equivalent of rafting down the Colorado River after flying around in the Grand Canyon. These monolithic pinnacles look particularly awesome from the bottom. This trip is available during the calm surf conditions of the summer months (May through September) and occasionally in winter when the ocean allows it. All year, water tours of the southern shores are available and, from January through April, whale watching in this region

Zodiacs brave rough winter waters on the Nā Pali Coast.

SHORT EXCURSIONS

There are four basic types of boat trips: by small power cruiser, by power-driven inflatable raft (usually called Zodiac, a brand name), by sailboat and by kayak. At least one company, NaPali-Kauai (826-7254, 800 367-8047) offers power cruiser, sailboat and Zodiac options. The most popular of these options is the Zodiac. The most experienced operator is Na Pali Zodiac (826-9371), better known as Captain Zodiac. Not all the tour guides and pilots are equally experienced, however (this is a job popular with California youth), and the bits of Hawaiian 'history' related by some of them are quite creative and original. If you have a choice, go with a guide who is mature and native to the island, or at least to Hawai'i. Tours offered by other operators, such as **Blue Odyssey** (826-9033), are very similar to Captain Zodiac's, but Na Pali Zodiac is the only Zodiac operator with permission to land, and they do so on their all-day and 'ultimate' trips, for lunch, snorkeling and onshore exploration at Nu'alolo Kai or Miloli'i State Parks—both with beaches that are inaccessible except by sea. There are about a dozen Zodiac operators based on the North Shore, and most of them take passengers into sea caves—when ocean conditions permit—and sometimes under waterfalls.

Zodiacs, however, are not for everyone. They are fun, but the ride can be rough, is almost assuredly wet, and there are no restroom facilities on board. For those preferring a drier, smoother ride, cabin cruisers are the answer. Popular operators of these are **Lady Ann Cruises** (245-8538, 800 367-8047 x446), leaving from Hanalei, and **Na Pali Kai Tours** (800 445-6142), leaving from Nāwiliwili and Port Allen (335-5044) year-round and from Hanalei (826-9011) May through October. An excellent and unusual Nā Pali tour is the all-day excursion run by **Playtime Charters** (335-5074), which leaves from Port Allen on the South Shore and travels around the western side of the island. This narrated hour-and-a-half journey provides a novel perspective and includes information about Ni'ihau, which can be seen on the horizon; it is followed by a standard three-hour picnicking, snorkeling and sightseeing cruise along the Nā Pali Coast. The cabin cruisers as well as the Zodiacs enter the huge vertical lava tube and the horseshoe-shaped sea cave, except when the sea is too rough.

Most North Shore tour companies also offer South Shore snorkeling and whale-watching expeditions during the winter months when the surf pounds the North Shore with twenty- to thirty-foot waves. In addition, **Captain Andy's Sailing Adventures** (822-7833) offers sailing/snorkeling excursions, sunset sails and seasonal whale watching along the south coast aboard a twenty-four-foot catamaran.

For a delightfully different experience, **Island Adventure** (245-9662, 800 331-8044) runs kayak tours up the Hule'ia River, off Nāwiliwili Harbor, passing the famous Alakoko (Menehune) Fishpond, and visiting the upstream filming sites of the movies *Raiders of the Lost Ark* (where Indiana Jones swung from the vines of a 'South American' jungle) and *Uncommon Valor* (where Gene Hackman thrashed his way through the thick tropical forests of 'Vietnam'). A midstream picnic and swim stop breaks the journey, which is followed by a short, narrated hike through a forest area of the Hule'ia National Wildlife Refuge offering interesting insights into Kaua'i's natural environment, then a van ride back to the starting point. The craft used are 'royaks', a cross between a kayak and a canoe, and anyone can paddle them easily after a few minutes' practice.

On the east coast, a relaxed, tranquil cruise up the broad, winding Wailua River is one of Kaua'i's most popular visitor activities. These tours, run by **Smith's Motor Boat Service** (822-4111) and **Waialeale Boat Tours** (822-4908) visit the famous Fern Grotto, with narration on the upstream leg and Hawaiian entertainment downstream. Smith's, the granddaddy of Wailua riverboat cruises (since 1947), also offers a twilight trip, a visit to the Fern Grotto by torchlight and candlelight and a floating lu'au.

EXTENDED CRUISES

American Hawaii Cruises (550 Kearny Street, San Francisco, CA 94108 800 227-3666) operates seven-day cruises around the Hawaiian island chain, stopping at Kaua'i's Nāwiliwili Harbor. They run the two historic, thirty thousand-ton sister ships, SS *Constitution* and SS *Independence*, built in 1951. The Constitution was re-christened in 1982 by Her Royal Highness Princess Grace of Monaco, who sailed aboard the ship in 1956 with her wedding party. The two ships were refurbished in 1980 and have been serving Hawai'i ever since.

They occasionally make trans-Pacific voyages between Honolulu and Seattle, Los Angeles or San Francisco, but are usually found cruising warm Hawaiian waters. Starting from Honolulu, the ships make similar rounds visiting the islands of Hawai'i, Kaua'i and Maui, with ports of call at Hilo, Kona, Nāwiliwili and Kahului, where they cross paths. Shipboard accommodations—cabins, staterooms and suites—range in size, location and price and determine the overall cruise fare. Besides an abundance of food, entertainment and recreational facilities, the optional, planned activities on board and shore excursions will keep energetic passengers bustling.

Typical tropical mood.

Land tours

There are only a few options for getting around on land. Buses come in several varieties; numerous types of private vehicles can be rented; there are two horseback tour companies and one bicycle tour company; and, of course, there are lots of places to go on foot.

GUIDED GROUP BUS TOURS

Huge buses that hold half a hundred people or more are good for keeping large tour groups together, and they are air-conditioned. Several smaller sizes of bus are also used by tour companies and these, though not always air-conditioned, afford a more intimate atmosphere for the passengers. Best of all are the increasingly popular mini-buses or large vans that are used by many local tour companies. These allow the most personalized service of all. **Trans Hawaiian Kauai** (245-5108) offers many different routes to most popular destinations. **Chandler's Kauai Tours** (245-9134) uses vans to transport small groups of sightseers to the full gamut of localities, offering an excellent selection of both short and long excursions. **North Shore Cab** (826-6189) does run a taxi service, and they also offer a short historical tour of the North Shore and an all-day tour from Princeville to Hānāpepe. **Kauai Island Tours** (245-4777), **Gray Line-Kauai** (245-3344) and **Robert's Hawaii** (245-9558) can accommodate those interested in the general sightseeing routes on buses of various sizes and vans.

Most tour operators offer reduced prices for children. Advance reservations should be made for all tours; most hotels have courtesy desks in their lobbies where these can be arranged quickly and easily.

FOUR-WHEEL DRIVE

A unique tour experience is that offered by **Kauai Mountain Tours** (245-7224), the only operator licensed to go into Kōke'e State Park. They travel roads that wind through the forest and down the back of Waimea Canyon, occasionally fording streams along the way; and the well-informed narrative enhances appreciation of the surrounding environment. A picnic lunch prepared by the Green Garden Restaurant is another highlight of this all-day tour.

LIMOUSINE

If you prefer a private excursion, there are limousines at your service, at hourly rates. **Limo Limo Limousine Service** (822-0393) has a range of Cadillac limousines and stretch limousines, plus a grand white classic Rolls Royce, and can arrange gourmet picnics and other special touches on request. **Kauai Island Tours** (245-4777) offers personal, private tours in late-model Cadillac sedans.

MOPED

You can motor along on two wheels for a more casual, outdoor touring experience. Renters of mopeds must be licensed and over the age of eighteen. Those not holding major credit cards must leave substantial cash deposits.

Pedal & Paddle (826-9069) in Hanalei, **Rent-A-Jeep** (245-9622) in Līhu'e and **South Shore Activities**

(742-6873) in Po'ipū rent these low-powered, slow-moving scooters. Mopeds are very popular with young beach-going visitors in particular. Drivers of mopeds should be especially aware of other vehicles and should move to the side of the road allowing cars and trucks to pass. They should also avoid bumpy surfaces and loose gravel.

CAR RENTAL

Kaua'i has a dozen car rental agencies, so you will be able to get a car if you want one. Most of the agencies provide current standard American and Japanese sedans and compacts, and some have convertibles, station wagons, even vans. Most are automatic with air

Warm winds, calm waters, and exquisite isolation.

conditioning, but standard shift, non-air-conditioned vehicles are available for the budget-minded traveler. In addition to the driver's license requirement, renters of cars must be at least twenty-one years of age; those under twenty-five must also hold a major credit card.

Budget Rent-A-Car, along with global giants Hertz and Avis have facilities at both Lihu'e and Princeville Airports. Hawai'i's own Tropical Rent-A-Car joins them with Dollar Rent A Car, Alamo Rent A Car, National Car Rental, United Car Rental, Thrifty Rent-A-Car and Rent-A-Wreck, which rents slightly damaged used cars. Rent-A-Jeep specializes in jeeps and other four-wheel drive vehicles.

BICYCLE

Traffic is generally light and poses little hazard to alert cyclists, and pedaling along under your own steam provides an even closer experience of the natural beauty of Kaua'i's tropical enviroment.

A unique bicycle tour of Kaua'i's rural North Shore is offered by North Shore Bike Cruise & Snorkel (822-1582). The cycling part of this all-day excursion covers about six miles, from the Wainiha area to the end of the road, with narrration all along the way, and is followed by snorkeling and hand-feeding the fish, and a barbecue picnic on the beach. All equipment is provided and child-size bicycles and baby seats are available. The pace is leisurely and well-suited to family groups.

Touring bicycles can be rented from South Shore Activities (742-

6873) in Po'ipū, and from Pedal & Paddle (826-9069) in Hanalei. If you need emergency repairs, Bicycle John (245-7579) and Kauai Sports (245-8052) in Lihu'e, and Bicycles Kauai (822-3315) and Kawamoto's (822-4771) in Kapa'a offer service in a half-day to a day, depending on the problem.

For further information and handy hints about cycling in Hawai'i contact the Hawaiian Bicycling League (PO Box 4403, Honolulu 96822).

HIKING

The most intimate look at the world around you can, of course, be got by walking slowly through it and keeping a sharp lookout. For self-guided hikers, there are many wonderful hiking trails detailed under Hiking in SPORTS.

There is, however, on Kaua'i an unusual hiking opportunity. Local boy Lloyd Pratt, himself an avid hiker, has created Local Boy Tours (822-7919), and offers a wide range of guided hikes requiring varying levels of exertion, visiting such natural settings as beaches, waterfalls, lava tubes, canyons and forested uplands, and lasting from a half-day to a whole day with longer camping excursions by special arrangement. Shorter tours can also be tailored to your interests. These excursions are accompanied by a treasure trove of legend and natural history from Pratt, who has been exploring this island on foot all his life and whose intimate knowledge of his island is accompanied by a deep love for it.

EXPLORING

Sightseeing
Historic sites
Parks and gardens
Beaches

SIGHTSEEING

K aua'i has a splendid array of sights worthy of visitor attention. Descriptions follow a counterclockwise sequence around the island. Be on the lookout along the roads for the Hawai'i Visitors Bureau 'Hawaiian warrior' signs that indicate points of interest and other places.

SCENIC AREAS

There are few places in Hawai'i that are not scenic—especially on Kaua'i—so we here draw attention to some of the more spectacular natural features. Details of historic sites and buildings, museums, sacred sites, parks and gardens are included under specific subheadings in this section.

The most famous area of this beautiful island is its spectacular **Nā Pali Coast**, an awesome array of perpendicular cliffs and eroded pinnacles punctuated by waterfalls and hanging valleys that end abruptly in sheer palisades at the sea. The best known of these valleys is **Kalalau**, which can be reached via an eleven-mile, cliff-hugging trail that traverses several smaller valleys along the way.

Above Kalalau are a couple of spectacular viewpoints, **Kalalau Lookout** and **Pu'u o Kila Lookout**, reached by road from the other side of the island, that afford breathtaking vistas. Alternatively, they offer the fascinating experience of watching a cloud coming, being surrounded by it, and watching it

Some of the island's best hiking is found on the Nā Pali Coast.

pass on, sometimes filling the valley entirely then, as it disperses, dramatically unveiling the scene four thousand feet below. The lookouts and the surrounding forest preserve are located in **Kōke'e State Park**, adjacent to the **Alaka'i Wilderness Preserve**, and the thirty-square-mile **Alaka'i Swamp**, the natural drainage sump for **Mount Wai'ale'ale** and the source of most of the island's rivers and streams.

The second most famous natural feature on Kaua'i is the colossal **Waimea Canyon**, touted by tourist literature as the 'Grand Canyon of the Pacific'. Some credit Mark Twain with this quote; others claim he never set foot on this island. In any case, the canyon—twelve miles long and three thousand feet deep—is spectacularly beautiful and, though hardly comparable to that great chasm of the American Southwest, is still high on the list of the world's magnificent sights. It is especially awesome when considered in relation to the size of the island. Near its mouth, just above the town of Waimea on the island's southern shore, are the remains of **Kīkī a Ola** or the **Menehune Ditch**, an irrigation canal and a prodigious feat of ancient engineering. The remaining ruins are located, not at all conspicuously, at the end of Menehune Road, in Waimea off Kaumuali'i Highway.

At the far end of the road on the western shore is **Polihale State Park**, a long strip of sandy beach tucked at the base of sheer gray cliffs, with Ni'ihau and its offshore islet, Lehua, visible across the Kaulakahi Channel. The park contains the ruins of two *heiau* and a sacred spring. The last five miles of the access road is unpaved and can become boggy in wet weather.

Though there were a few villages

Hanalei Bay is subject to strong currents during winter months.

along this coast in ancient times, the nearest town is now Kekaha. Here Mānā Road (550) turns off Kaumuali'i Highway (50) then becomes Kōke'e Road and climbs twenty miles to Kokee Lodge and Kōke'e State Park. Also numbered 550 is Waimea Canyon Drive, which starts at Kaumuali'i Highway in Waimea and meets Kōke'e Road about halfway up the mountain. It is strongly recommended that you take one route up and the other down as the views from each are magnificent and quite different.

It was at Waimea that Captain Cook first made landfall in the Hawaiian Islands, in January 1778,

of Hanapēpē town at the sign pointing toward the Veterans Cemetery; drive past the cemetery then west on Lokolai Road until you can see them. East of Hanapēpē, a Hawai'i Visitors Bureau warrior marks a scenic overlook into the **Hanapēpē Valley**. This is a vista worth stopping for.

Just west of Kalāheo, you will find the turnoffs leading to **Kukui o Lono** (*makai* of the highway on Pāpālima Road), the former estate of Walter McBryde, encompassing a Japanese garden and a nine-hole golf course, and **'Olu Pua Botanical Gardens** (*mauka*, directly off the highway), a former plantation

Kīkī a Ola, the Menehune Ditch.

and there is a monument to him in the middle of town. On the eastern bank at the mouth of the Waimea River stand the ruins of **Fort Elizabeth**, built by Russians in 1816.

Near Hanapēpē, between the Port Allen Airport and Salt Pond Beach Park are the ancient **Salt Ponds**. There are no signs to lead you there. Turn *makai* off Kaumuali'i Highway (50) just west

manager's estate and gardens.

Not far east of Kalāheo, a turn *makai* onto Kōloa Road (530) will take you, after a short distance, to Hailima Road (an inconspicuous fork) and the Visitor Center of the **Pacific Tropical Botanical Garden**, a tropical plant research facility. Farther down Kōloa Road, you will arrive at Old Koloa Town, where another turn *makai* will take you past Kūhiō Park to the **Spouting Horn**. There are holes in this coastal shelf where the force of waves under the rock causes water to spurt into the air, but one waterspout shoots far higher than the others. On a mildly windy day with a small ocean swell, it has been seen to go as high as thirty to forty feet.

Taking Maluhia Road (520) north from Old Koloa Town, you will drive through Kaua'i's famous **Tunnel of Trees**, rows of huge swamp mahogany whose branches meet overhead 'in a continuous leafy canopy. Along Kaumuali'i Highway (50) just west of Puhi, there is a warrior marker indicating **Queen Victoria's Profile**, which some say can be discerned in the outline of the Hā'upu Range (now often called the Hoary Head Range) to the south. She's supposedly looking eastward.

At the eastern edge of Kukui Grove Center, just west of Līhu'e, a turn *makai* onto Nāwiliwili Road (58) will take you to **Nāwiliwili Harbor**. Only about a hundred yards *mauka* of the terminus of this road, on the eastern side, is the entrance to the **Menehune Gardens**. Nāwiliwili Harbor and Kalapaki Beach can also be reached by following Rice Street through Līhu'e. Going west at Nāwiliwili

Waimea Canyon--an anomaly in the Hawaiian Islands.

Harbor on Wa'apa Road, you will see the Hawai'i Visitors Bureau marker for the **Menehune Fish-pond;** turn *mauka* onto Hulemalū Road. At the top of the hill is a scenic lookout over this ancient aquacultural structure, known to Hawaiians as **Alakoko.**

Following the same road past the harbor and straight into Līhu'e, on Rice Street you will pass the Kaua'i Museum. Only a little farther along the same route is the junction of Kaumuali'i (50) and Kūhiō (56) Highways. Straight ahead on Kaumuali'i and just past the underpass, a Hawaiian warrior marker indicates the Ho'omana Road turnoff to the **oldest Lutheran Church** in the state of Hawai'i, built in 1883.

A turn at the Līhu'e junction onto Kūhiō Highway leads to Kapaia where Mā'alo Road (583) turns *mauka* and leads to a scenic overlook of **Wailua Falls.** Kūhiō Highway continues through Hanamā'ulu to **Wailua,** the home base of Kaua'i's

ruling chiefs prior to European settlement of the island. Stone remnants of ancient buildings abound in the area. On the coast between Wailua Golf Course and the Wailua River Bridge, is **Lydgate State Park,** where the ruins of Hauola Pu'uhonua and Hikina a Kalā Heiau stand in a coconut grove. Along the southern bank of the river, *mauka* of the bridge are Wailua Marina and **Smith's Tropical Paradise,** a botanic garden.

Across the bridge and just *mauka* of Kūhiō Highway on Kuamo'o Road (580) is the Coco Palms Resort with its famous coconut grove, and a little farther along the road on the opposite side are Holoholokū Heiau and Pōhaku Ho'ohānau (Royal Birthing Stones). A little farther up the hill, just before the 'Ōpaeka'a Falls/Wailua River lookout, a dirt road on the left (opposite a public 'comfort station') leads to the ruins of Poli'ahu Heiau and continues downstream where a walkway leads to the **bellstone.**

A couple of miles up the hill, still on the same road (580) is the scenic viewpoint for **'Ōpaeka'a Falls.** On the opposite side of this bridge, there is a splendid view of the **Wailua River** and the tour boats going to and from the **Fern Grotto,** a pretty, fern-encrusted cavern farther upstream. The Grotto's flowers and ferns grow upside down

Misty mountain rainbow.

Princeville is made up of private homes, condominiums and golf courses.

from the top of the cave, and after a look inside, visitors are serenaded with the 'Hawaiian Wedding Song'. It is also, as the song suggests, a popular site for weddings. From the bridge, you also look down upon **Kamokila Hawaiian Village**, an excellent reconstructed facsimile of the village that once stood on the site; the entrance to Kamokila is immediately adjacent to the western (*mauka*) end of the bridge.

Nounou Ridge, the mountain spur behind Wailua has the profile of a reclining man and is known in legend as the **Sleeping Giant**. North of Wailua, Kūhiō Highway (56) passes the huge Market Place at Coconut Plantation on the edge of Waipouli before entering Kapa'a, the largest town on the island. At the north end of town, there is a **scenic lookout** over Keālia Bay. Between here and the North Shore are a lot of cane fields. About halfway between **Anahola Bay** and

Moloa'a Bay there is a scenic lookout, and at the Moloa'a Road turnoff, there is an excellent fruit stand well worth a refreshment stop.

Several miles farther along Kūhiō Highway, you come to the small town of **Kīlauea**. Perpendicular to the charming little church made of lava rock is Lighthouse Road. A couple of blocks along a small street called Oka, on your left, leads to the famous Jacques Bakery. A little farther down Lighthouse Road, you pass the Kong Lung Co. store—a very old store, established in 1892, with a very modern range of exclusive merchandise—and the Lighthouse Gallery behind. At the end of Lighthouse Road is Kīlauea Lighthouse, now within the **Kīlauea Wildlife Refuge**. Kaua'i's rugged Kīlauea Point is a favored nesting site for large colonies of Red-footed Boobies, Wedge-tailed Shearwaters, and other species.

The Fern Grotto has long been a popular wedding site.

Just west of Kīlauea is a scenic lookout over **Kalihiwai Bay,** followed by the Princeville Airport. Continuing westward be on the lookout for Banana Joe's fruit stand with its frozen fruit whips. A couple of miles farther, on the left, you can't miss the entrance to the Princeville resort community, which contains condominiums and private homes, many available for short-term rental; one of the island's two largest golf courses (thirty-six holes); and the Sheraton Princeville Hotel. Immediately past the shopping center, on the opposite side of the road, is a scenic viewpoint providing a stunning vista of the beautiful **Hanalei Valley.** The road then winds sharply downhill to the picturesque old **Hanalei Bridge,** thence to Hanalei Town. A little farther westward, at Wai'oli, are the Waioli Mission Church and, behind it, the Waioli Mission House.

From here the road follows the shoreline quite closely—passing many beautiful beaches and is punctuated at frequent intervals by one-lane bridges over the many small streams running through this well-watered agricultural district. Especially quaint is the double bridge at Wainiha. West of Hā'ena are three ancient lava tubes known as **Maniniholo Dry Cave, Waikapala'e Wet Cave** and **Waikanaloa Wet Cave,** which, according to legend, were dug by the goddess Pele. Geologists prefer to believe that they were formed by wave action when the sea level was higher, some four thousand years ago. At the end of the road is **Kē'ē Beach.** Near the path from the beach to the *heiau* is a cottage where part of the movie *The Thornbirds* was filmed. Beside the parking area at the end of the road is a large sign marking the beginning of the Kalalau Trail into the valleys of the **Nā Pali Coast.**

Waimea Canyon, early morning.

HISTORIC SITES AND BUILDINGS

For ancient Hawaiians, virtually all natural features of the landscape had meaning. In a culture rich with oral tradition, the symbolic significance of every cave, crater, pinnacle and headland was passed from generation to generation, giving life and immediacy to the historic and mythic legends of gods and heroes. This abundant lore fills volumes, but here we offer a sampling to provide a glimpse of the way the Hawaiians of old related to the land that nurtured them.

Kaua'i's folklore is especially rich with tales of the Menehune (see IN-TRODUCTION), and these tiny people are held responsible for many of the natural features of the landscape as well as for some otherwise unexplained man-made structures. The most outstanding and well known of the latter are Kīkī a Ola or the Menehune Ditch at Waimea and Alakoko or the Menehune Fishpond on the Hule'ia River at Niumalu. Kīkī a Ola was an irrigation canal that brought water from high in the Waimea Canyon to the taro patches of the ancient village of Waimea. The cut and keyed stonemasonry demonstrates both knowledge and tools of a technology the Hawaiians of Cook's day did not have, so the artisans' identity remains a mystery. This sort of stonework is found nowhere else in the Hawaiian islands. Alakoko is a nine hundred-foot-long wall cutting off a bend in the river to create an enormous pond for raising and harvesting fish. Such ponds were common along the coasts of all Hawaiian islands, but the size and stonework of this one is exceptional.

Pōhaku Ho'ohānau or the Royal Birthing Stones, located near Holoholokū Heiau in Wailua, is a consecrated grouping of large stones where *ali'i* women were brought to give birth ceremonially, with the appropriate *kāhuna* in attendance, in order to assure the highest *mana* for their offspring. If the newborn were male, the nearby bellstone was rung to announce his arrival; females entered the world unannounced.

The mountain ridge behind Wailua is the form of a Sleeping Giant named Nounou. He sleeps for centuries at a time and gets all covered with dirt and trees grow on him. People forget about him and have, it is said, been very frightened when he wakes, but he is a friendly fellow who has helped the local people with such tasks as transporting stones from one side of the island to the other and building *heiau*. Exhausted from his labors and full after a feast given in celebration of his last completed work, he lay down again for another few centuries of deep slumber.

The fire goddess Pele is said to have come north from the land of Kahiki in search of a new home. Her route of migration took her right across the Hawaiian Islands, and everywhere she went, she thrust her digging stick into the ground looking for an appropriate homesite. On Kaua'i's North Shore are the results of three unsuccessful attempts—Maniniholo Dry Cave, Waikapala'e Wet Cave and Waikanaloa Wet Cave—before she moved on across the archipelago, finally finding what she was looking for in the Big Island's Kīlauea Firepit, where she still lives and regularly reminds residents of her presence.

There are also sites of more recent historic interest. Near Ku'unaka'iole Point at Hanapēpē are the ancient **Salt Ponds** where Hawaiians flooded clay beds with sea water and, after evaporation, collected the crystals. They still do, and posted *kapu* signs warn intruders to keep their distance. Locals much prefer the flavor of this salt, red from the residue of clay it contains, over the commercial variety, but it cannot be sold as it does not meet government standards of purity.

A park on Lāwa'i Road between Kōloa and Kukui'ula (the route to Spouting Horn) marks **Kahoai**, the **birthplace of Prince Jonah Kūhiō Kalaniana'ole**, born on March 26, 1871, to High Chief David Kahalepouli Pi'ikoi and Kinoiki Kekaulike. After the overthrow of Hawai'i's monarchial government, Kūhiō served as Hawai'i's second elected representative in Washington, DC from 1902 until his death on January 7, 1922.

On the north bank of the Wailua River, a couple of miles upstream from the ocean, stood a village whose remains were uncovered in the 1930s by a farmer, Ben Ohai. Aware of the significance of the site and of the fading of Hawaiian culture, he made it his life's work to excavate and recreate that village as an educational site. Though he did not live to see the dream realized, his family has carried it out and the village, now named **Kamokila**, meaning 'stronghold', offers Kaua'i visitors and residents alike the closest thing they're ever likely to see to an ancient Hawaiian village. For those who have visited remote villages on South Pacific islands, where Polynesian culture still

The ruins of Russian Fort Elizabeth.

thrives, Kamokila Hawaiian Village feels like a time warp, its authenticity a palpable presence. Demonstrations of food preparation, crafts and ancient games are also included. (M-Sa 9am-4pm admission 822-1192)

At the mouth of the Waimea River stand the ruins of **Fort Elizabeth**, built by Russians in 1816 in an unsuccessful attempt to gain a foothold in the Islands to serve as a strategic and secure base of supply for their outposts in Alaska and the northwest coast of North America. The plans of Dr Georg Anton Scheffer, their commercial agent, who carried out this scheme, were disavowed by the Tsar, and Kaumuali'i, still ruler of the island, was chastised by Kamehameha I, to whom he had pledged his loyalty. The wall of the Fort originally sloped directly to the river, but

home has now been restored and converted to commercial use except in the living room and dining room, which have been retained with their furnishings, many of them the originals, to illustrate the gracious lifestyle of the former residents.

George Wilcox founded Grove Farm Plantation in 1864, and ran it from **Grove Farm Homestead**. The original plantation house, added to in later years, is still there, along with the plantation office, guest and workers' cottages, worksheds, flower and vegetable gardens, fruit orchards and more. The Wilcox family occupied this home continuously for more than a century, until Miss Mabel Wilcox, who was born on the property, died in 1978 at the age of 96. Prior to her death she planned the present use of her eighty-acre estate, establishing a non-profit educational organization to maintain Grove Farm Homestead and Waioli Mission House, and to preserve, study and interpret the history of missionary and plantation life on Kaua'i. Miss Wilcox and her sisters also collected, over the period of their lifetimes, an outstanding collection of Hawaiian quilts, which have been preserved in exceptionally good condition and are

Waioli Mission House Museum.

subsequent siltation has created a ledge in front of it.

Kilohana was built in 1935 by Gaylord and Ethel Wilcox of Grove Farm Plantation, one of Kaua'i's largest sugar growers. Unoccupied and unattended for many years, the

kept at Grove Farm. A beautifully illustrated book—*The Wilcox Quilts in Hawaii*—describing these, the people who made them and the people who collected them, is available at the office.

Mabel Wilcox and her sisters

Ethel Wilcox and Etta Sloggett, are also responsible for the preservation and restoration, in 1921, of **Waioli Mission House** at Wai'oli, near Hanalei, the former home of their grandparents, Abner and Lucy Wilcox, missionary teachers who came to Kaua'i in 1846. Shipped around Cape Horn from Boston in 1836, in pre-cut pieces, this typical two-story New England cottage was erected by Reverend William Alexander, Kaua'i's first missionary preacher, and was subsequently occupied by the Wilcox family until it became a museum. Much of the original furniture was and still is in it, preserving the flavor of nineteenth-century missionary life in this remote corner. (Tu & Sa 9am-3pm 826-6447)

The fifty-two-foot **Kīlauea Lighthouse**, built in 1913, boasts the world's largest clamshell lens, the moving parts of which weigh four tons. An electronic beacon, installed in front of the lighthouse in 1976, has superseded the massive lamp, which completed a revolution every twenty seconds, turning on a mercury float, flashing ten thousand candlepower seaward every ten seconds. In clear weather this light has been seen from as far as ninety miles out to sea. Still operated by the US Coast Guard, the lighthouse is now within the Kīlauea Point Wildlife Refuge. (grounds open M-F 10am-4pm; scenic overlook provides view at all times)

MUSEUMS

The **Kōke'e Natural History Musem**, located next to Kokee Lodge in Kōke'e State Park houses displays of the plant and animal life of Kaua'i and the other Hawaiian islands, and an excellent three-dimensional map of Kaua'i.

A permanent exhibit at the **Kaua'i Museum** tells the story of Kaua'i—or as much of it as is known—from its formation as a single volcanic island some sixty million years ago, up until the nineteenth century and the development of the sugar plantations. An excellent continuous loop film gives an overview of Kaua'i today; ask at the desk about purchasing a cassette of its superb soundtrack. Another wing of the museum houses local artifacts and temporary exhibitions, generally of very high quality, that change every few months. The Museum Shop carries a very good selection of books and gift items related to the natural and cultural history of the island. (M-F 9:30am-4:30pm Sa 9am-1pm 4428 Rice Street, Līhu'e 245-6931 admission)

At the **Hanalei Museum**, the term is very loosely applied. An old building containing a miscellaneous assortment of local memorabilia and old photographs, this collection is charming in its ingenuous genuineness, and offers a dusty glimpse of the neighborhood's past that is not represented elsewhere. Augmented by a two-table snack shop, it's an interesting step off the beaten path. (Kūhiō Hwy, Hanalei 826-6783 donation). Virtually across the street, in the building entitled Native Hawaiian Trading and Cultural Center, is the **Native Hawaiian Museum**, a single room containing an honest and admirable attempt at displaying examples of the tools and technologies of Hawaiians in the pre-European era.

HEIAU

The sacred structures where Hawaiians ceremonially honored their gods are known as *heiau*. The remains of many of these can be seen, though some have been completely destroyed in the clearing of land for alternate use, and others are shrouded in dense thickets of overgrowth. Though official use of all *heiau* ceased more than a century and a half ago, fresh offerings are often found at the ruins. As these sites are still considered sacred by many of Hawai'i's people, please treat them with due respect, keeping them clean and leaving all stones in place.

Those most likely to be encountered by visitors are in the Wailua area, the seat of power for Kaua'i's ruling chiefs before European contact. At the mouth of the Wailua River, on the south bank in a coconut grove lie the ruins of **Hikini a Kalā Heiau** and, adjacent to it, those of **Hau'ola Pu'uhonua**, an ancient place of refuge for offenders who had broken *kapu*, or warriors who had been defeated in battle. If they could reach a *pu'uhonua* [place of peace] before their pursuers could catch them, they were safe and, after a period, could return to society. Beside the river are several boulders carved with ancient petroglyphs; these are sometimes covered with sand and difficult to detect. Just *mauka* of Kūhiō Highway (56), on Kuamo'o Road (580) lie the ruins of **Holoholokū Heiau**. This former *luakini* is on the left, right beside the road. The stone slab in the far corner was the sacrificial altar.

Only a few yards farther along the roadside are the Pōhaku Ho'ohānau or the Royal Birthing Stones, a consecrated site where *ali'i* women gave birth. Farther up Kuamo'o Road on the lefthand side, shortly before the lookout for 'Ōpaeka'a Falls, a dirt road leads to the ruins of **Poli'ahu Heiau** and continues downstream where a walkway leads to the **bellstone**, one of a group of boulders, which, when struck in a precise way at a particular spot, gives a clear ringing tone. According to tradition, this signal was sounded to announce the birth of male *ali'i* at the *pōhaku ho'ohānau* down the hill. It is not now known which of the stones was used or how to tap it to produce a sound that carries for an appreciable distance. Many people try their hand, however, and as a result, the stones have been badly damaged and are being gradually chipped away. Visitors to the site are asked to refrain from hitting the stones.

Archaeologists are currently preparing a program of interpretation for the area. The other important *heiau* in the area, **Malae Heiau**, is in the middle of a cane field and all overgrown so it cannot, at present, be visited with ease.

There are two other *heiau* in accessible places. On the South Shore, **Kihahōuna Heiau** sits right on Poi'pū Beach, in front of the Waiohai Hotel and slightly to the east; it can also be reached from the west via Po'ipū Beach Park.

On the North Shore above Kē'ē Beach, which lies at the very end of the road, stand the ruins of **Kaulu Paoa Heiau** and, above that, the ancient site of a *hālau hula* [hula school]. The hula platform at this site is still used by local *hālau*, and is regularly cleaned and maintained by them.

Offerings left at Hauola Pu'uhonua.

PARKS AND GARDENS

Nā Pali Coast State Park encompasses some of the significant eastern valleys of the Nā Pali Coast wilderness. The best known of the valleys is **Kalalau**, east of Nu'alolo, where the remains of terracing and irrigation are most extensive. This wide valley ends at a long, lovely beach, in summer; much of the sand is removed by the raging winter surf and redeposited each spring. Access to Kalalau is also possible by an eleven-mile trial, that snakes its way up and down along a ledge hugging the cliffs. Built by the Hawaiians many centuries ago, the second valley is four miles farther along, the trail passing through a couple of small valleys—Ho'olulu and Waiahuakua—along the way. Hanakoa, a very rainy place, also has a lovely waterfall. Another five miles of steep, narrow trail, passing through another small valley called Pōhakuao, bring the intrepid adventurer at last to Kalalau Valley, with its pools, falls, ancient ruins and abundant legends, perhaps the favorite of which is that of Ko'olau the Leper. A native of Kekaha on Kaua'i's South Shore, Ko'olau contracted leprosy and in 1889 was

Gleams at play with Waimea mountains.

trail is very popular today with hikers and backpackers, but it is not for the casual stroller or the faint of heart. Starting from the end of the road at Ka'ilio Point, the trail passes through two other large valleys on its way to Kalalau—**Hanakāpī'ai** and **Hanakoa**. The former is two miles along the trail—a steep mile up and a steep mile down. At the back of this valley is a splendid three-hundred-foot waterfall. The scheduled for transportation to the Kalaupapa settlement on Moloka'i. As the boat set sail without his wife and child, who he was promised could accompany him, Ko'olau realized that he had been tricked and jumped overboard, swimming ashore. With his family he hid in Kalalau where a number of lepers sought to evade the authorities. After a year, all the lepers in the valley were persuaded to leave,

except Ko'olau, who outmaneu-
vered a sheriff's posse and a
subsequent detachment of the
National Guard, killing or wound-
ing several of them in the process.
Left alone, Ko'olau and his wife
(their son also contracted the
disease and died quickly) lived in
the valley for another five years
until he died and she buried him
there. Ko'olau has become something of a local folk hero.

The hanging valleys, ending in
sheer cliffs at the sea, which lie
farther westward along this coast,
are now described as 'inaccessible',
but they were inhabited and
extensively terraced by large groups
of Hawaiians in the many centuries
of occupation prior to the arrival of
Europeans in the Islands. As the
culture and values changed, the
difficulty of access to these valleys
became a burden and they were
abandoned, but remains of *lo'i* [taro
terraces], irrigation channels, *heiau*
and house foundations are still
evident beneath the overgrowth.
The largest population, sometimes
dramatically referred to as the 'lost
tribe', occupied three large valleys—**Honopū, Awa'awapuhi** and
Nu'alolo—and six smaller ones. At
Nu'alolo there is a beach below the
sheer cliffs where canoes landed.
Access to the valley above was by

Late afternoon sun shadows the Nā Pali Coast.

means of a rope ladder. There was also a small permanent settlement known as Nu'alolo Kai (the valley above was Nu'alolo 'Āina) nestled against the cliffs at the back of the beach, and the stone remains of this village can be visited by boat. The beach area is now **Nu'alolo Kai State Park**, and only two *tour* boats are licensed to land here. A little farther westward along the coast is another beach, **Miloli'i State Park**, below the Koahole Valley and accessible only by private boat.

A few miles down the west coast of the island is **Polihale State Park**, a hot, dry area popular for its long sandy beach and its sunset views, the color dramatically reflected by the high, rocky cliffs in the background. The area was special to the Hawaiians of old, and the park contains the ruins of two large *heiau*—**Kapa'ula Heiau** and **Polihale Heiau**—and a sacred spring. Access is from the end of

the highway via five miles of graded dirt road, which can become impassable for ordinary cars in very wet weather.

Around the curve of the island on the south coast is the mouth of the Waimea Canyon, stretching twelve miles up into the island's interior. Some 1866 acres of the chasm's upper reaches are designated **Waimea Canyon State Park** and are contiguous with **Kōke'e State Park**, encompassing 4345 acres of the island's upland wilderness and affording unsurpassed opportunities for exploring an unspoiled natural environment. The Parks' nature trails vary greatly in length and difficulty, offering something for virtually everyone. Adjacent to Kōke'e State Park is the **Alaka'i Wilderness Preserve**, encompassing the Alaka'i Swamp, at ten miles long and two miles wide, approximately the size and shape of Manhattan. Entry into the

The clouds' dramatic unveiling of Kalalau Valley.

swamp's upper reaches is restricted, but hiking into parts of it is permitted. Altogether there are forty-five miles of wonderful nature trails—for both vehicles and hiking—in this area.

For the casual stroller, the delights of nature can be greeted at one of Kaua'i's several botanic gardens. **'Olu Pua Botanical Gardens**, off Kaumuali'i Highway half a mile west of Kalāheo, was founded in the 1900s as a plantation manager's estate of the Kauai Pineapple Company. Its twelve and a half acres have been converted to a private botanical garden with an active, ongoing collecting program to expand the diversity of plantings, which already include tropical vegetation from around the world. Narrated tours of the grounds provide ample information about the many types of trees, flowers, vines, shrubs and other plants. (tours M-W-F 9:30am, 11:30am,

1:30pm reservations 332-8182 admission)

Kukui o Lono, also at Kalāheo, is another private estate now open to the public. In addition to a beautifully-landscaped Japanese garden, complete with torii gate and Oriental garden sculpture, Walter McBryde, the sugar plantation heir who founded the estate in the 1900s, imported and planted some fifty thousand shade and flowering trees, and went around the island collecting stones of legendary and mythical significance to the Hawaiians, which he removed to his estate garden. These include Kaua'i Iki [small Kaua'i], a large, flat stone shaped like the island; the eye of the anchor, which held Ni'ihau to Kaua'i; Pohanuhuna'ahu'ula [a feather cape stone] where kings hid their royal cloaks to avoid detection; and others, plus stone bowls, salt pans and tree molds formed by lava flows. McBryde also arranged to

Polihale Beach, still considered a sacred place by many.

have himself plated in the garden upon his demise, and his grave is flanked by two stone lions. Adjacent to the garden is a nine-hole golf course.

Kaua'i's 186-acre **Pacific Tropical Botanical Garden**, dedicated in 1971, was chartered by the US Congress as a tropical plant research center, the primary function of which is the increase of scientific knowledge. The world's tropics contain vast numbers of unstudied species, even undescribed species, and new ones are continually being discovered.

As part of its educational role, the Garden conducts guided tours twice daily, but numbers are strictly limited and advance reservations are essential. The Monday through Friday tours also include the gardens of the adjacent Allerton estate, an exquisite haven started in the 1870s by Queen Emma, wife of Kamehameha IV. The Visitor Center, at the end of Hailima Road (off Kōloa Road) is open daily from 7:30am to 4pm. (reservations 332-7361)

Menehune Garden in Līhu'e offers guided walks along its meandering paths past lots of interesting tropical flowers, shrubs and trees, the most notable of which is a sprawling Chinese weeping banyan, planted in 1896, that spreads its branches over about an acre, even though Hurricane 'Iwa removed a chunk of it in 1982. (off Nāwiliwili Road, just north of the harbor 245-2660)

Smith's Tropical Paradise is spread across thirty acres along the south bank of the Wailua River, with its entrance next to the Wailua Marina. Attractively landscaped, it offers a suggested route or you many find your own way amongst

the labeled specimens of native and introduced tropical foliage with pseudo-Polynesian and Filipino structures and a huge head meant to resemble those stone monoliths from Easter Island scattered about for added interest. A garden in the middle of the pond is graced by a Japanese garden. A lu'au is held here nightly with a show in the amphitheatre. Tram rides around the park are available for an extra fee. (daily 8:30am-4:30pm 822-4654 and 822-9599)

Wailua River State Park encompasses 1126 acres of the Wailua River and its banks up the South Fork to Wailua Falls and up the North Fork past 'Ōpaeka'a Falls to Koholālele Falls, including **Lydgate State Park** on the coast near the mouth of the Kauai Resort. The River Park contains the remains of several *heiau* and other culturally important sites as well as the popular tourist destination, the Fern Grotto. The Beach Park contains the ruins of a *heiau* and associated *pu'uhonua* .

Kīlauea Point National Wildlife Refuge on Kaua'i's rugged Kīlauea Point is a nesting site for large colonies of Red-footed Boobies and Wedge-tailed Shearwaters; and other species such as the Red-tailed Tropicbird, the Laysan Albatross and the Great Frigatebird are also often seen here. A Visitor Center adjacent to Kīlauea Lighthouse has displays explaining Hawai'i's seabird sanctuaries and the birds they protect. It is interesting to note that seagulls do not nest in the islands.

Hā'ena State Park, a sixty-two-acre beach park on the north coast where camping is extremely popular, is detailed in BEACHES and ACCOMMODATION.

BEACHES

Kaua'i is blessed with sweeping strands of pristine sand along most of its coast. Ocean recreation was an important facet of life for the ancient Hawaiians, and remains a major feature of island life, for visitors as well as residents. Many island visitors come from inland areas and are unfamiliar with the awesome power of the sea and with the vagaries of its personality. For all its beauty, it must be approached with respect and caution; and then it provides a great deal of pleasure. This section contains information relevant to beach activity—including warnings—followed by descriptions and ratings of Kaua'i's beaches.

WARNINGS

Heed all warning signs posted at beaches. Lifeguards are stationed at only two of Kaua'i's beaches—Po'ipū and Salt Pond—and many of this island's beaches are steep and have very strong ocean currents especially in winter when high surf is usual. Recorded information on current surf conditions around the island is available on 245-6001.

Many visitors spoil their vacations by spending too much time in the sun in the first day or two. The sun in Hawai'i is much harsher than in more northerly (or quite southerly) climes. This calls for sunblock for all but the most acclimatized and dark-skinned individuals. Limit

51

Taking it easy at Po'ipū Beach.

your time in the sun to an hour or so the first day—depending on the fairness of your skin. You can increase this by ten or twenty minutes a day as you gradually develop a tan.

One of the gravest potential dangers of the deep is the caprice of waves. 'Typical' wave action varies with the local shoreline and the season. On Kaua'i's North Shore the sheer size of the winter surf is dangerous, with waves cresting up to thirty feet. The surf on the eastern and western shorelines can also be high in winter. In summer, high seasonal surf can occur off the south shore.

Shorebreaks are places on or near the shore where incoming ocean swells cross abruptly from a deep to a shallow bottom and the waves break with enormous downward force. Though they are dangerous for swimmers, these beaches are popular as they provide excellent conditions for body surfing. It is well, though, to know how to deal with them. Neck and back injuries can be sustained, and turning your back on or trying to jump over or through a large incoming wave invites trouble. The force of the wave can pound you against the bottom, knock your breath away and cause you to lose your sense of direction. The trick is to take a deep breath and dive *under* the wave.

Another potential danger at such beaches is the backwash, water which has been washed onto the shore and must run back again to the sea. On steep beaches, or after the arrival of particularly voluminous waves, the force of this water can be almost as powerful as the incoming wave and can sweep a person off his or her feet and out to deeper water.

This water rushing back to the sea sometimes gets trapped by other incoming waves and can build to a considerable volume. When this happens, the only way it can move is sideward, creating a rip current that runs along the beach until it finds a deeper bottom. If you find yourself caught in a rip, the best course of action is to flow along with it until its force diminishes. Don't exhaust yourself trying to swim against it. It's easier and safer to walk back along the beach to the place where you started than to fight the water. Some rip currents flow straight out to sea through channels in the reef. If you are caught in one of these, swim to the side of it to get out. This type of rip is far more dangerous.

Sometimes this backed-up water cannot find an outlet and must flow back out *under* the incoming wave. This creates the condition known as undertow. An undertow is a brief phenomenon, lasting only until the wave has passed. For a person pulled down in an undertow, a few seconds under water can seem much longer. Remain calm and come up for air on the other side of the wave.

Another potentially dangerous wave action is the collision of deep ocean swells with rock ledges. It is never safe to venture out to the edge of rocks where surf is breaking. Freak waves can wash over the rocks without warning and many unsuspecting people have been swept away by such waves.

Underwater ledges, too, can present some danger from the surprise of a sudden dropping away of the bottom. Very shallow water can become very deep without notice, so non-swimmers should always keep away from such areas.

Crystal clear Hāʻena Point at the end of the road.

A sunset walk along Po'ipū Beach.

RATINGS

We have rated the beaches according to our interpretation of the following criteria: water safety, bottom configuration (sand, rock, coral), cleanliness/maintenance of beach area, and type and quality of facilities (restrooms, showers, picnic tables, barbecue pits, parking). This is naturally arbitrary as not everyone feels the same about what's most important in a beach. All of Kaua'i's beaches are beautiful, though many are washed by very strong currents. Symbols denote beaches that are especially good for board surfing ●, body surfing ● (includes body boarding), windsurfing ●, snorkeling ●, and swimming ●. Seasonal variances are also noted. These are VERY important as they relate primarily to safety.

The ratings and descriptions of beaches are arranged in geographical order around the island in a counterclockwise direction, starting on the western shore.

Superb	★★★★
Excellent	★★★
Good	★★
Fair	★

1 Polihale
2 Barking Sands
3 Kekaha
4 Waimea

● Body Surfing   ● Board Surfing   ● Windsurfing   ● Snorkeling   ● Swimming

1   Polihale   ★★   ● (winter, expert only)

Fringing the edge of Polihale State Park is a wide expanse of white sand that stretches unbroken all the way to Kekaha—about ten miles. The Park is at the very end of the road, the last five miles of it unpaved. The Nā Pali Coast starts (or ends) here. Above the beach tower spectacular gray cliffs. Ni'ihau and Lehua can be seen on the horizon, and here the sun sets directly into the sea. Unobstructed by fringing reefs, the waves roll in with full force, making even summer water conditions unsafe for swimmers, and the severe winter surf is recommended only for expert surfers. There is a natural pool called Queen's Bath about midway down the Park's shoreline, south of the parking lot, which affords safe summer swimming. *Follow the State Park signs from the end of Kaumuali'i Hwy (50).*

2   Barking Sands   ★

This sandy beach is wide, and surf and water conditions here are similar to those at Polihale. Public use of the beach at the Barking Sands Missile Range is allowed when there are no military maneuvers in progress (335-4111). *Access is through the military reserve and visitors must sign in at the gate.*

3   Kekaha   ★★★   ●●●

This long, wide stretch of sand along the southwest coast is a continuation of the beach that starts beneath the cliffs at Polihale. Though it is subject to strong currents and surf from both southern summer and western winter storms, it can have safe conditions at any time of year (call 245-6001 for information). *Access is directly off Kaumuali'i Hwy (50).*

4   Waimea   ● (summer)

What has been erroneously called Waimea Black Sand Beach in some guidebooks is really just a muddy shoreline. The sand is black from dirt washed down the Waimea River and is not volcanic black sand, as are some of the

Fleeting fantasy kingdom.

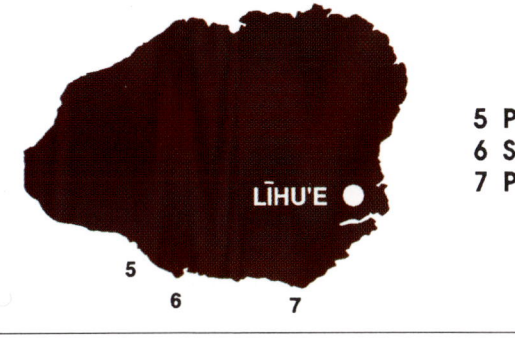

5 Pākalā
6 Salt Pond Beach Park
7 Po'ipū Beach Park

LĪHU'E

5

6   7

● **Body Surfing**   ● **Board Surfing**   ● **Windsurfing**   ● **Snorkeling**   ● **Swimming**

beaches on the Big Island. The water is also murky with suspended soil particles. The fishing pier here is very popular and there is good summer surfing offshore. *Turn* makai *just west of the Waimea River Bridge.*

5 Pākalā ☆ ●● (summer)

Located off the main highway and reached via a path through a cane field, this secluded curve of sand, rendered bronze by runoff from the rich red earth beyond, is divided by a rocky promontory. The water is shallow and murky from soil runoff, and the bottom is rocky, making swimming conditions unpleasant. The offshore surfing break here, known as 'Infinities', is considered one of the best summer surfing spots in all Hawai'i. *Park beside Kaumuali'i Hwy (50) on a wide sandy area beside a low concrete bridge near the Mile 21 Marker.*

6 *Salt Pond Beach Park* ★★★★ ●●

A semicircular band of gently sloping golden sand and a protective fringing reef make this one of the island's most popular swimming beaches. Persistent patterns of fair weather add to its appeal. Showers, restrooms, picnic tables and barbecues facilitate family outings, and there are lifeguards on duty daily, year-round. Some of the ancient saltpans nearby are still used by locals to harvest sea salt, and tidal pools harbor interesting little sea creatures. *At Hanapēpē, turn* makai *at the sign pointing to the Veterans Cemetery, then right onto Lolokai Road.*

7 *Po'ipū Beach Park* ★★★★ ●●●● (summer)

Another fairly long stretch of wide, sandy shoreline with a sloping sandy bottom, this is generally a good swimming beach, with stronger wave surges in summer providing bodysurfing conditions. Lifeguards are on duty daily, year-round. Showers, restrooms, picnic tables, pavilions, barbecues and a children's playground are available in the Park, and anyone is free to use the beaches fronting the hotels. An area past a rocky point at the eastern end of the beach—generally known as Brennecke's—make the area dangerous for any wave riding. *Follow Maluhia Road (520) or Kōloa Road (530) to Kōloa Town then take Po'ipū Road* makai *to the coast.*

8   Shipwreck   ☆ ●● (summer)

This pretty stretch of unshaded beach is washed by strong currents and surf and is fringed by a rocky shelf that spoils its potential as a swimming beach, but some body surfers use it in summer and it is popular year-round with windsurfers. *Access is via the dirt road that continues past the paved portion of Po'ipū Road, then a right (makai) turn at the first opportunity.*

9   Māhā'ulepū   ☆☆ ●●

Though all beaches in Hawai'i are public up to the high-water mark, land access to this lovely stretch of shaded sand is possible only by crossing private land. The western end is protected by a fringing reef, creating calm waters for swimming and snorkeling, but the area is subject to strong currents and high summer surf. *About two miles east of Shipwreck Beach; low cliffs along the shoreline prevent walking from one to the other.*

10   Kīpū Kai   ☆☆☆ ●●

Accessible only by water, this pretty, isolated beach with a gently sloping sandy bottom is a favorite spot for boat outings, particularly during winter when high surf conditions prevent the popular boat trips down the Nā Pali Coast (see Water Tours under GETTING AROUND).

11   Kalapakī   ☆☆☆ ●●●● (summer)

This is the 'town beach', in front of the Westin Kauai Hotel and adjacent to Nāwiliwili County Park. The beachfront has a gently sloping sandy bottom and the sheltered cove affords good swimming, windsurfing and body surfing all year and, occasionally in summer, even board surfing. *At the bottom of Wa'apā Road, Līhu'e.*

12   Hanamā'ulu   ☆ ●

The beach here is a crescent of soft sand, with a gradually sloping sandy bottom, but Hanamā'ulu Stream, which empties into the bay, makes the water murky and poor for water activity. There are restroom, shower and picnic facilities and the area is popular for camping. *Turn makai off Kūhiō Hwy (56) at Hanamā'ulu, bear right at the fork and follow the road to the end.*

13   Lydgate State Park   ☆☆☆ ●●

Though this stretch of coastline is subject to strong currents and dangerous winter surf, lava rock walls have been built at this popular beach park to break the force of the waves, creating two areas—one shallow enough for small children—that are safe for swimming all year. When the sea is calm, snorkeling is good outside the breakwater, but powerful currents at the river mouth make swimming here risky at all times. The park has all the facilities for family outings, and interesting ruins of a *heiau* and *pu'uhonua* lie in the coconut grove.

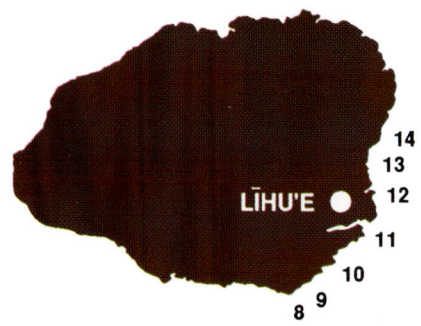

8 Shipwreck
9 Māhā'ulepū
10 Kīpū Kai
11 Kalapakī
12 Hanamā'ulu
13 Lydgate State Park
14 Wailua

LĪHU'E

● Body Surfing ● Board Surfing ● Windsurfing ● Snorkeling ● Swimming

Access is off Leho Drive, which is a loop that joins Kūhiō Hwy (56) just north of the Wailua Golf Course and just south of the Kauai Resort Hotel.

14 Wailua ★★ ●● (winter)

Unprotected by fringing reef, this stretch of wide, sandy beach is washed by strong currents all year and, in winter when ocean swells run higher, the area is popular for surfing, but water conditions for swimmers are quite dangerous. *Access directly from Kūhiō Hwy (56), across from Coco Palms Resort.*

Romantic evening skies, Hanalei.

15 Kapa'a ★ ●

A small reef about twenty yards offshore protects the Kapa'a shoreline from the full force of ocean swells, but the beaches are eroded and narrow and the bottom shallow and rocky, making swimming conditions poor. Snorkeling is okay in calm conditions. *Access directly off Kūhiō Hwy (56).*

16 Keālia ★★ ●● (summer, cove only)

A popular surfing spot, this long, wide beach has a sheltered cove at the north end where swimming is safe in summer. Interesting tide pools at the southern end attract marine biology students as well as the casually curious. *Access directly off Kūhiō Hwy (56).*

17 Donkey Beach ★★ ● (winter)

Access to this isolated beach, where water conditions are dangerous is across private land. Permission to pass through may be requested during business hours at the office of Lihue Plantation at 2970 Kele Street (beside the Post Office), Līhu'e. *Access off Kūhiō Hwy via the second cane haul road past the Mile 11 Marker north of Keālia.*

18 Anahola Bay ★★★ ●● (summer) ●● (winter)

At the eastern end of the bay, Anahola Beach County Park has showers, restrooms, picnic tables and barbecues, and a protecting reef offshore makes water conditions safe for summer swimming, but high winter surf can create surges and currents hazardous to swimmers. Winter wave conditions are strongest around the center of the beach with gentler surf at the northern end.

19 Moloa'a Bay ★★★ ●● (summer)

Tucked into the northeastern edge of the island, this bay is off the beaten path, reached by a winding rural road. The long, wide beach is fronted by a fairly steep sandy bottom, and during heavy surf, there are dangerous currents. *Kūhiō Hwy (56) to Moloa'a Fruit Stand, just south of Kīlauea; left on Kuamo'o Road then right on Moloa'a Road to the end; walk along the path, crossing the shallow stream.*

20 Larson's Beach ★

Though there is an offshore fringing reef, this beach has amongst the most treacherous water conditions on the island and swimming here at any time is risky; in winter it is out of the question. This beach is, though, a beautiful, isolated spot, and is favored by beachcombers and *limu* [seaweed] pickers. *Access is off Ko'olau Road which joins Kūhiō Hwy (56) at both ends. The turn is makai onto a dirt road which is about a mile from either end; the straight road to the beach is marked.*

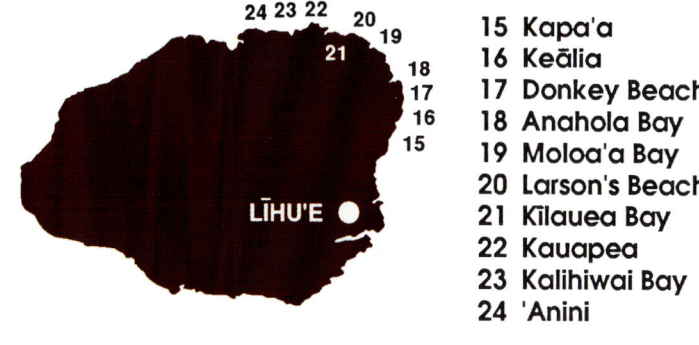

24 23 22 20 19
21
18
17
16
15

LĪHU'E ●

15 Kapa'a
16 Keālia
17 Donkey Beach
18 Anahola Bay
19 Moloa'a Bay
20 Larson's Beach
21 Kīlauea Bay
22 Kauapea
23 Kalihiwai Bay
24 'Anini

● **Body Surfing** ● **Board Surfing** ● **Windsurfing** ● **Snorkeling** ● **Swimming**

---

21 *Kīlauea Bay* ☆ ● (winter) ● (summer)

Difficult to get to, Kīlauea Bay has a shallow sandy bottom and is safe for swimming on very calm days in summer, but treacherous in winter when high surf rolls right in. *Access is via a long, badly-rutted dirt road off Kīlauea Lighthouse Road, the second right past the Kong Lung Co. store.*

22 *Kauapea* ☆ ●● (winter) ● (summer)

So far off the beaten path that it is sometimes referred to as 'Secret Beach', this secluded stretch of sand lies at the base of a cliff just west of Kīlauea Point and can be reached only by hiking down. Wide in summer, the beach may almost disappear under the pounding waves of winter surf. Currents are unpredictable. *Access is via a dirt road just a few yards west of Kolo Road (the entrance to Kīlauea Town); turn makai off Kūhiō Hwy (56) and follow the road until it ends. A sign marks the beginning of the beach trail.*

23 *Kalihiwai Bay* ☆☆ ● (summer) ● (summer) ● (winter)

This lovely curved bay with a shallow, sandy bottom offers calm and gentle waters in summer and formidable high surf in winter—in common with the north shores of all Hawaiian islands. *There are two separate intersections of Kalihiwai Road with Kūhiō Hwy (56); the beach can be reached from either end.*

24 *'Anini* ☆☆ ●● (summer)

This county beach park has showers, restrooms, and picnic facilities, but the beach itself stretches for a couple of miles and is usually almost deserted. The water is too shallow for swimming, though snorkeling is good. Even in winter when the rest of the North Shore is dangerous, this beach and its inshore waters are sheltered by a fringing reef that is the largest in Hawai'i. *Access is via 'Anini Road, a turn west off the western section of Kalihiwai Road, which runs makai off Kūhiō Hwy (56) almost opposite the Princeville Airport.*

25 Hanalei Bay ★★★★ ●● (winter, expert only)

This perfect, curved bay, legendary for its beauty, is subject to dangerously strong currents even in summer, especially around the center of the bay, and to raging surf in winter. Swimming is safe year-round at both extreme ends of the bay. *Access is via Aku Road or Weke Road, both* makai *turns off Kūhiō Hwy (56) at either end of Hanalei Town.*

26 Lumaha'i ★★★★ ●● (winter, expert only) ● (summer, far eastern end only)

This long, wide strip of sandy shoreline is amongst the most beautiful—and most photographed—beaches in the world, and is best known for its starring role in the movie *South Pacific*. Unfortunately, no fringing reef protects its inshore waters, and the beachfront is totally exposed to the full force—and caprice—of the ocean. A river flows past the western end, and when the *muliwai* (estuarine pond) is closed off from the ocean by a sandbar, swimming here is safe. *Access at the western end is directly off Kūhiō Hwy; at the eastern end, a trail descends a steep, muddy slope (there is no marker, but you will see lots of cars parked along the road).*

27 Wainiha ★

This beach is beautiful and usually fairly empty because its steep foreshore and strong currents make water activity here dangerous. It is, nonetheless, an excellent spot for sunning and picnicking in pristine solitude. The Wainiha River flows to the sea at the western end of the beach. *Access is directly off Kūhiō Hwy.*

28 Hā'ena ●● (winter)

There are three distinct sections to the long stretch of Hā'ena Beach, each of which has different inshore conditions. All are popular for windsurfing year-round. Winter conditions afford the best wave jumping and are for experts only. The same goes for board riders of the huge winter waves.

At the eastern end, known by the name of its offshore surfing break, **Tunnels** ★★★★ ●● (summer), the beach is wide and sandy and the bottom sandy with a gentle slope. There are patches of rocky reef in the shallow inshore waters, but there is plenty of room around them for good summer swimming. Winter wave conditions are gentler at this end of the beach. Farther westward along the beach is **Hā'ena Beach Park** ★★ ● (summer), a county facility that is popular for camping. Swimming is dangerous in winter, when surfing is good. This center section of the beach is not nearly as nice as the two ends. The western end of the beach, again known by the name of its offshore break, is called **Cannons** ★★★ ● (summer). A little steeper than the beach at Tunnels, the backwash here is stronger, but swimming is safe on a calm summer day, and this end of the beach is usually sparsely populated. *Access to Tunnels is via a sandy road off Kūhiō Hwy (56) exactly 1.1 miles west of Charo's Restaurant; otherwise, access is directly from the highway.*

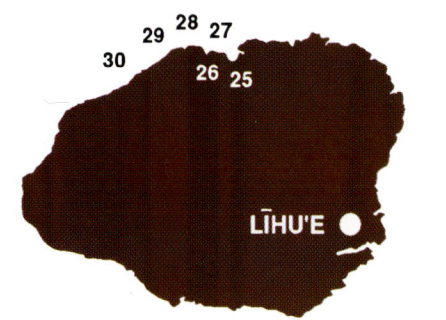

25 Hanalei Bay
26 Lumaha'i
27 Wainiha
28 Hā'ena
29 Kē'ē
30 Nā Pali

● Body Surfing   ● Board Surfing   ● Windsurfing   ● Snorkeling   ● Swimming

Sunset fades on the South Shore.

29   Kē'ē   ★★★ ●● (summer)

This small, lovely curve of beach is fronted by a gently sloping sandy bottom in fairly shallow water, calm and protected for swimming, surrounded by patches of reef that are excellent snorkeling grounds. *This is the end of the road; the beach is next to the small parking lot, which also is the starting point for the Kalalau Trail into the valleys of the Nā Pali Coast.*

30   Nā Pali   ★ ●● (winter, expert only)

Tucked into the cliffs along this precipitous coastline are beaches at **Hanakāpī'ai** and **Kalalau,** which are accessible via the Kalalau Trail (see Hiking under SPORTS). These are largely ripped away by ocean currents during the high surf of winter and redeposited in spring. Accessible only by boat are the beachheads at **Nu'alolo Kai** ●● (summer) and **Miloli'i** ●● (summer) **State Parks** (see Water Tours under GETTING AROUND). *Extreme caution should be exercised at these wilderness beaches as there is no help nearby in case of emergency.*

SPORTS

Scuba diving
Windsurfing
Golfing
Hiking

SPORTS & RECREATION

Prior to the arrival of Europeans Hawaiians had developed a variety of sports and games and have always been enthusiastic sportsmen. Traditional sports and games are too numerous to detail here. The ones still popular today are surfing—which has spread to many parts of the world—and outrigger canoe racing, though they have been substantially altered from the way they were done in ancient times. Hawaiians also took readily to many of the sports introduced by various immigrants to these islands, and today the people of Hawai'i participate in a wide cross section of recreations and competitive events. Favored snorkeling and surfing areas are noted in the BEACHES section. Phone numbers and addresses of sports equipment rental companies are listed at the back of this book .

SNORKELING

Snorkeling provides excellent and easy access to the underwater world for swimmers curious about submarine scenery.

Snorkels, masks and fins are available from **South Shore Activities** in Po'ipū, **Aquarius Beach Center** at Coconut Plantation Marketplace in Kapa'a, **Beach Activities of Kauai** at the Sheraton Princeville, **Princeville Video & Beach Rentals** at Princeville Center, and **Pedal & Paddle** in Hanalei, and at all the dive shops listed below. All operators of water tours provide snorkeling equipment as part of the package. Underwater cameras are available for rental from **Dive Kauai** in Kapa'a, **Ocean Odyssey** at the Kauai Hilton in Waipouli, Beach Activities of Kauai, Princeville Video & Beach Rentals and Pedal & Paddle.

Good snorkeling areas are denoted by the symbol ● in the BEACHES section of this book.

SCUBA DIVING

Take a tank dive for an even deeper look at Kaua'i's undersea environment. Certified divers may rent equipment and go out on their own, or may arrange a chartered excursion. Those unfamiliar with local conditions are encouraged to take an escort as this sport is potentially dangerous, even for trained divers. Introductory classes are available for those seeking certification. Dives take place wherever conditions are best at the time; this generally means the North Shore in summer and the South Shore in winter, as this is the prevailing pattern of calm waters. Depths range from twenty to a hundred and fifty feet, with most areas falling into the middle of that spectrum.

Though there is good shore diving along much of Kaua'i's coastline, most of the island's top dive spots are accessible only by boat. Some very good diving is found off the Polihale coast in the area known as **Mānā Crack**. Several interesting sites lie off the southwest coast. Near Kukui'ula Bay, a site with the popular name **General Store** is the location of a nineteenth-century shipwreck, and two caverns are home to a large variety of colorful tropical fishes. Off Ka'ūlala Point, **Oasis Reef**, a solitary pinnacle surrounded by sand, attracts lots of fishes, octopi, lobsters and moray eels. Near Nahumā'alo Point, ledges and holes of the lava terraces at **Fishbowl** attract an excellent variety of fish which like to be hand-fed. Off Po'ipū, three large, parallel lava tubes collectively known as **Sheraton Caverns** form one of Kaua'i's most popular dive spots. One

Some interesting coral types also grow here, and whitetip reef sharks occasionally visit the area. The reef areas off Lihu'e Airport offer three good dive spots. Near Nāwiliwili Bay, **Aquarium** has a good variety of both corals and fishes as well as several cannons from an eighteenth-century shipwreck. An unusual formation called **Dragon's Head** is named for its appearance; many of its caverns contain rare black coral and large fish such as *ulua* [jack crevalle] and rays frequent the area. There are also lots of crustaceans under ledges and in holes.

Kaua'i's oldest boat harbor, **Ahukini Landing** (now unused), is

Ideal dive spots ring Kaua'i's coastline.

shelters a lobster nursery; all are frequently visited by large turtles and, occasionally, by whitetip reef sharks. The reef off Brennecke's Beach drops off sharply, creating **Brennecke's Drop**, a long ledge with many holes and overhangs where turtles frequently sleep.

popular for introductory dives and has a good variety of fish as well as interesting coral formations such as the unusual plate coral. Off the cliffs of the Princeville coast, the awesome drop-off of **Do Drop In**, has large formations of many types of coral including trees of black coral, and abundant reef fishes. For experts only is the spectacular dive of **Oceanarium** where tall pinnacles and sheer, deep drop-offs display excellent coral formations and attract large fish such as barracuda, rays and *ulua*. The only one of the island's dozen top dive spots accessible from the shore, **Cannon's Reef** lies off the western end of Hāʻena Beach. Turtles are common in the area, and whitetip reef sharks can be found cruising the long ledge or sleeping in caverns formed by lava tubes. There are also good diving spots along the Nā Pali Coast. Because of high winter surf conditions, North Shore sites are diveable only in summer.

Kauaʻi's dive tour companies include **Fathom Five Professional Divers** (742-6991) and **Kauai Divers** (742-1580) in Kōloa, **Ocean Odyssey** in Waipouli, and **Aquatics Kauai** (822-9213), **Sea Sage Diving Center** (822-3841) and **Wet-n-Wonderful Ocean Sports** (822-0211), all in Kapaʻa. All give instruction for certification to varying levels and some do night dives. Sea Sage, Dive Kauai and Ocean Odyssey also rent underwater cameras, and Ocean Odyssey or Wet-n-Wonderful will, for the same price, take your photos or videos for you, with you in them. Dive Kauai has prescription masks for those who need them. Scuba lessons are also available from the beach service concessions in Poʻipū, at the Sheraton-Kauai, Kiahuna Plantation and Waiohai Hotels and near Brennecke's—**Sea Sports Kauai** (742-1221), **Kiahuna Beach Hut** (742-6411), **Waiohai Beach Service** (742-7051) and **Brennecke Ocean Sports** (742-6570).

Snorkeling satisfies the most curious of visitors.

SURFING

Since these island-based people lived constantly within reach of the sea and its changing waves, it is not surprising that Polynesians invented the sport of surfing. While many other Polynesian groups enjoyed riding surf in their outrigger canoes, Hawaiians alone developed the art of riding boards specifically designed for play atop the rolling waves.

In modern times, this ancient sport has been refined and extended beyond anything its inventors ever imagined and its popularity has spread around the globe, professional surfers demonstrating their skill and daring while vying for six-figure purses. The manufacture of surfing equipment and accessories has become a major industry. Several types of board surfing have also developed as well as, in recent years, the new variant: surf sailing or windsurfing. The areas best suited to these various types of surfing are noted in the BEACHES section.

Board surfing

This is the original. No one knows how long ago it developed, but Hawaiian petroglyphs dated to about the eighth or ninth century show people board surfing, and as early as the fifteenth century, Hawaiians had so refined the sport that contests between champions were held—for what even we would consider to be high stakes. Ancient Hawaiians gambled with unbridled enthusiasm at every possible opportunity, wagering their property, their wives, even their lives on the outcome of a single game. Many famous surfing exploits were passed down through the voluminous oral history of these people. Their name for what we call surfing was *he'enalu* which can be loosely translated as 'wave sliding' but which, like everything else in the Hawaiian language is rich with a range of subtlety and poetic nuance that says much more. The best surfing breaks were reserved for use by the ruling chiefs and violators of this *kapu* could be punished by death.

Surfing, like all things Hawaiian, declined dramatically during the first century or so of European immigration to the Islands, but surfing—both on boards and in canoes—began to be promoted again in Hawai'i early this century. Surfing's international fame began to spread with the demonstrations in Atlantic City and Australia that were given by surfing champion and Olympic gold medal swimmer Duke Kahanamoku.

The original boards were eighteen-foot, hundred-and-fifty-pound monoliths, often made of koa. This began to change in the mid-1940s with the development of hollow boards and ones built of such lightweight materials as balsa and redwood, then fiberglass and synthetic foam. The evolution of surfboards has also seen a wide variety of lengths, widths and thickness, and these variations on the theme have been found to excel in varying conditions so that, today, top surfers keep collections of several boards from which to choose.

The beach services at the

Sheraton-Kauai, Kiahuna Plantation and Waiohai Hotels and near Brennecke's in Po'ipū—**Sea Sports Kauai, Kiahuna Beach Hut, Waiohai Beach Service** and **Brennecke Ocean Sports**—rent surfboards and give surfing lessons, as does **Beach Activities of Kauai** at the Sheraton Princeville, in winter. **Garden Island Windsurfing** (826-9005) also offers surfing lessons.

Surfboard rentals are available from **South Shore Activities** in Poi'pū, **Kalapaki Beach Center** at Nāwiliwili in Līhu'e, **Wailua Surf & Beachwear** in Wailua, **Aquarius Beach Center** at Coconut Plantation Marketplace in Kapa'a, **Aquatics Kauai** and **Sea Sage** in Kapa'a, **Princeville Video & Beach Rentals** at Princeville Center, **Sand People** and **Pedal & Paddle** in Hanalei.

Body surfing

This is a cross between board surfing and swimming and stems from the same principle as board riding except that the body replaces the board as the vehicle. The ancient Hawaiians called this activity *kaha nalu* or *pae* or *paepo'o*. There are two basic techniques for accomplishing this feat: keeping the body straight with the arms pinned against the sides while riding the shoulder of the wave just ahead of the breaking water, and the alterna-tive of keeping one or both arms straight out in front for greater maneuverability. The former technique seems to work best in offshore breaks while the latter seems best in the large, shallow shorebreaks. Most expert bodysurfers use both, sometimes while riding the same wave. Though purists decry it, virtually all bodysurfers also use fins to increase propulsion and enhance their ability to catch a wave.

Paipo boarding

The term paipo is a post-World War II corruption of the Hawaiian *paepo'o*, and, essentially, is a 'bellyboard'. This type of wave-riding board is short and thin—three or four feet long and only a quarter to half an inch thick—either flat or with a slightly concave surface to fit the body. They are mostly homemade and mostly used by Hawaiians. Their use requires skill and they have been largely superseded in popularity by the now well-known 'Boogie ® board'.

Body boarding

The body board, developed from the paipo board described above, was invented in Hawai'i in the early 1970s by Tom Morey, and is made of flexible foam. The 'boards' are a couple of feet wide, about four feet long and around three inches thick and, like their parent paipo, are ridden prone. The latest development along this line is a high performance body board—now termed 'turbo board'—that was invented by Russ Brown in 1983. Considered the Porsche of body boards, it is stiffer and faster than the standard model. These inexpensive water toys have become ubiquitous in Hawai'i, and are readily available for rental or sale all over the island.

Some of the places you can find them are: **South Shore Activities** and the beach service concessions at the Sheraton-Kauai and Waiohai Hotels and near Brennecke's in Po'ipū, **Progressive Expressions**, **Fathom Five Professional Divers** and **Kauai Divers** in Old Koloa Town; **Ocean Odyssey** at the Kauai Hilton in Waipouli; and **Sea Sage**, **Aquatics Kauai** and **Dive Kauai** in Kapa'a.

Sand sliding

This, too, is an ancient pastime that has been given a modern tool. The original idea was to throw oneself onto the sand at the precise moment when a receding wave had left just a thin sheet of water on which the body would then slide. Precise timing was—and is— essential as too early a leap results in a mere sinking to the sand and too late a one ends in an abrupt, abrasive halt.

Bare-body sand sliding is seldom seen anymore, but paipo boards and the more recent body boards are also used in this fashion. Nowadays the hot trend is the 'skimboard', a short foam 'board' about three quarters of an inch thick that is thrown onto the receding wave then jumped upon.

Skilled standing riders have developed some fancy skateboard-like maneuvers on this type of board, and contests have been held on O'ahu. It can also be ridden as a 'bellyboard' in waves.

Surfing is not just a sport, but a way of life to some.

WINDSURFING

The most imaginative modern variation of the ancient sport of surfing was its hybridization with sailing, conceived in 1970 by Californian Hoyle Schweitzer and executed by his friend Jim Drake. The popularity of this new sport spread like wildfire and a circuit of amateur and professioanl contests is already well established. Windsurfing championships held for years on O'ahu have recently been canceled due to the Pro World Tour that has lured away all the big-money prize winners.

'Anini Beach is Kaua'i's best windsurfing spot because its waters are protected by Hawai'i's largest fringing reef and the prevailing northeast tradewinds blow fairly steadily onshore. These conditions also make it one of the easiest places to learn.

Windsurfing specialist **Action**
Windsurfing in Old Koloa Town offers sailboard rental and expert instruction, and **Kalapaki Beach Center** in Līhu'e also provides instruction with their rentals. **Garden Island Windsurfing** (826-9005), established as a top windsurfing school for the past decade, offers instruction at all levels at both North and South Shore locations. **Hanalei Sailboards** (826-9732) also offers expert instruction. The beach service concessions at the Sheraton-Kauai and Waiohai Hotels and near Brennecke's in Po'ipū rent sailboards and give windsurfing lessons. Sailboard rentals are also available from South Shore Activities in Po'ipū, **Wailua Surf & Beachwear**, **Aquarius Beach Center** in Kapa'a, **Princeville Video & Beach Rentals**, and **Watersports Kauai** and **Pedal & Paddle** in Hanalei.

SAILING

On whichever scale you choose—from small catamarans to large yachts—Kaua'i's waters offer exquisite sailing, with the North Shore in summer and the South Shore year-round being ideal for this activity. Small boats, such as Hobies, are available for anywhere from half an hour to all day. A good place for this service, and for
lessons if you're new to the sport, is **Pedal & Paddle** in Hanalei. In Po'ipū, the beach services—**Sea Sports Kauai** (742-1221) at the Sheraton-Kauai, **Waiohai Beach Service** (742-7051) and **Brennecke's Ocean Sports** (742-6570)—offer catamaran rides. For other adventures afloat, see Water Tours under GETTING AROUND.

KAYAKING

Now very popular in Hawai'i, this ancient Eskimo pastime translates well to the tropics. There are also canoe/kayak hybrids. **Island Adventure** (245-9662 or 800 331-8044) at Nāwiliwili runs two-hour
river adventures as described under Water Tours in GETTING AROUND and, on a charter basis, runs trips along the North Shore in summer and the South Shore in winter, as well as overnight

Kayaking to shore before a storm.

expeditions to other islands. Various kayaks and canoes can be rented from **Pedal & Paddle** in Hanalei, which also rents wave skis, a modern cross between a kayak and a surfboard with indentations for derriere and heels. Wave skis can also be rented from **Wailua Surf & Beachwear** and **Princeville Video & Beach Rentals**. Kayaks are also available from **Hanalei Sailboards**, and **Beach Activities of Kauai** at the Sheraton Princeville has 'glass-bottomed' kayaks.

WATERSKIING

The most popular place on the island for waterskiing is the broad, smooth Wailua River. The veteran operator here is **Kauai Waterski & Sports** (822-3574), who has been pulling skiers up and down the river for about fifteen years, also offering all levels of instruction. Rates are hourly. **Water Ski Kauai** (822-3388) has been around for a decade and also offers excursions at hourly rates, with free instruction if needed. **Adventures Unlimited Kauai** (245-8766) also offers hourly rates for skiing excursions, with lessons included when required.

JETSKIING and PARASAILING

Kauai Jet Ski Rentals offers hourly rentals, with instructions if needed, from Hanamā'ulu Bay. They prefer you to call first. **Adventures Unlimited Kauai** (245-8766) offers parasailing out of Hanamā'ulu Bay, taking six people at a time for an hour and a half, each person getting to spend about fifteen minutes aloft.

GLIDING

Kaua'i's only glider rides are available from **Sailplanes Kauai** (335-5446) operating daily between 9am and 5pm from the airport at Port Allen.

These deliciously silent aerial excursions carry two passengers at a time, and come in two varieties. One climbs to three thousand feet and takes about twenty minutes to descend, offering splendid bird's-eye views of the Hanapēpē Valley and the Salt Pond Beach area; the other climbs to five thousand feet, affording more distant views—of Kaua'i's east coast and of Lehua and Ni'ihau in the west. The longer descent takes around thirty to forty minutes. Reservations are recommended.

TENNIS

Almost every hotel and condominium complex on Kaua'i has courts, some of which may also be used by non-residents, with permission. The Kaua'i County Department of Parks and Recreation has public courts in Kekaha, Waimea, Hanapēpē, Kalāheo, Kōloa,

Līhu'e and Kapa'a; there is no fee for the use of these courts, but reservations (245-1881) are necessary. Additionally there are public courts at **The Waiohai Resort** (742-9511) and **Kiahuna Plantation** (742-6411) in Po'ipū, at **Coco Palms** (822-3831) in Wailua, **Tennis Garden** (826-9823) and **Hanalei Bay Resort** (826-6522) in Princeville.

GOLFING

Kaua'i has several excellent golf courses. The **Princeville Resort's** (826-3580) thirty-six holes of golf course designed by Robert Trent Jones, Jr, also augmented by a driving range, has been rated by *Golf Digest* among the 'hundred best' in America. The Westin Kauai's **Kauai Lagoons Golf and Racquet Club** (245-5050) in Līhu'e features thirty-six holes of Jack Nicklaus-designed golf course, overlooking Nāwiliwili Bay, and a driving range.

The **Kiahuna Golf Club** (742-9595) at Kiahuna Plantation Resort in Po'ipū has eighteen holes of Robert Trent Jones, Jr-designed golf course, plus a driving range. The nine-hole **Kukuiolono Golf Course** (332-9151), formerly part of the McBryde Estate in Kalāheo, is set in exquisite gardens and offers spectacular ocean views. The Kaua'i County Department of Parks and Recreation's **Wailua Golf Course** (245-2163) has eighteen holes and a driving range.

A relaxing horseback ride under sunny Princeville skies.

HORSEBACK RIDING

There are lots of scenic trailrides on Kaua'i, both along beaches and into the mountains. Excursions last from one to several hours, the longer ones including picnics.

Pooku Stables (826-6777) offers interesting explorations on the North Shore; South Shore rides are available from **CJM Country Stables** (245-6666).

HUNTING

Kaua'i has a lot of wilderness land where hunting is permitted, the most common quarry being feral pigs and goats, which are prolific and can be hunted, with varying restrictions, on weekends and holidays year-round. Black-tailed Deer can be taken during a limited period in early autumn. Pheasants, quail, francolin and doves can be hunted on weekends and State holidays only from November until the third week in January. Barred doves can also be taken on private land with the owner's permission during February and March and July through October, on weekends and State holidays only.

Maps of public hunting areas are available from the Division of Forestry and Wildlife (1151 Punchbowl Street, Rm 325, Honolulu 96813 548-2861 or 3060 'Eīwa Street, Līhu'e 96766 245-4433). All hunting requires a valid State of Hawai'i Hunting License; nonresident hunting licenses cost fifteen dollars and may be purchased from license agents at sporting goods stores or from the Division of Conservation and Resources Enforcement (1151 Punchbowl Street, Rm 330, Honolulu 96813 548-5918). For more information, contact one of these two State agencies.

FISHING

Freshwater fishermen must obtain licenses, but permits are not needed for recreational ocean fishing. Non-resident licenses cost seven dollars and fifty cents and may be obtained at any major sporting goods store or the Division of Conservation and Resources Enforcement office (1151 Punchbowl Street, Rm 330, Honolulu 96813 548-8766). The season is open year-round for most fish.

Kaua'i has many rivers and streams, but most are on private land and access can be problematic. Basically the same types of fish— tilapia, several kinds of bass, and a few types of catfish—were stocked decades ago into many of the reservoirs that dot the island, providing water for irrigation of sugarcane fields. These, of course, are also on private land, but if you enjoy tranquil boat fishing, **Bass Guides of Kauai** (822-1405) has

special arrangements with some of the South Shore plantations to allow private fishing parties. Up to three people at a time are taken for half-day fishing excursions to these otherwise unpeopled waters where a catch is almost a sure thing. All gear is provided, and pickup from East and South Shore locations can be arranged.

Shore fishing is popular at many places along the coast. Surf casting gear can be rented from **Yoshimura Store** in Kapa'a, and the friendly staff can also give you seasonal information about what fish can be found where.

Deep sea fishing lures a lot of enthusiasts to Hawaiian waters to catch *mahimahi* [dolphin fish] and, if lucky, *a'u* [marlin]. Kaua'i has a dozen companies offering sport fishing charters. **Kaulakahi** (337-1806) in Kekaha offers "extraordinary ocean experiences for the adventurous." **Sport Fishing Kauai** (742-7013) offers four-, six- and eight-hour trips, as does **Gent-Lee** (245-7504 or 337-1674), operating out of Nāwiliwili Harbor and **Seabreeze III** (828-1285) based at 'Anini.

Lucky Lady Charters (822-7033), **Alana Lynn Too Charter Fishing** (245-7446), **Adventures Unlimited Kauai** (245-8766) and **Coastal Charters Kauai** (822-7007) also operate out of Nāwilwili Harbor.

The Hawaiian Z-Boat Company (826-9274) takes fishing parties out from Hanalei Bay.

Reservations should be made in advance for these excursions; most trips can be arranged on a share basis or as private charters.

Aficionados know this is not an inexpensive pastime. Most operators keep at least some of the fish caught, and it's customary to tip the skipper and mate, especially if the catch is good.

HIKING

Kaua'i is a hiker's paradise. Very far from the madding crowd, most of the island remains in a natural state, primarily because so much of it is difficult to get to except on foot, and then only after considerable effort. The rewards are unparalleled views, many types of tropical vegetation, streams, waterfalls and swimming holes and, above all, exquisite isolation. There are long trails and short trails, easy trails and difficult—something to suit almost anyone.

The **Sierra Club, Hawai'i Chapter** (PO Box 11070, Honolulu 96822 946-8494) will, for a small fee, send an information packet describing state trails and trip-planning information. The Club's **Kaua'i Group** (PO Box 3412, Līhu'e 96766 822-7141 or 822-7654) welcomes visitors to join them on their regular hikes. The **Hawaii Trail and Mountain Club** (PO Box 2238, Honolulu 96804) is also helpful in providing information for hikers. The **Hawaii Geographic Society** (PO Box 1698, Honolulu 96806) offers books, maps and other publications and requests written inquiries from Hawai'i-bound

hikers. The **Hawai'i State Department of Land and Natural Resources, Division of Forestry** (1151 Punchbowl St, Rm 325, Honolulu 96813 548-8850) has free trail maps. Highly recommended is the inexpensive handbook *Hiking Kauai* by Robert Smith, which provides extensive and personally validated information on all the island's hiking trails.

Kaua'i's most extensive network of trails crisscrosses the upland forests and chasms of Kōke'e State Park, Waimea Canyon State Park and the Alaka'i Wilderness Preserve. Altogether there are twenty-eight named trails totaling forty-five miles in length through this unspoiled environment, rich in native flora and fauna, some of which is found nowhere else. A map of these is available from Kokee Lodge and in hiking books. For their own safety in the event of an emergency, hikers should sign out at Park Headquarters before setting out, and in again when they return. There are numerous wilderness campsites in the area.

In the southeastern quadrant of the island, an inland trek (2.5 miles)

Rocky shores mark the end of Polihale Beach.

to **Kilohana Crater** follows a cane haul road and leads to an abandoned house on the northeastern flank that was once a holiday retreat for pineapple plantation staff. The route passes working cane fields, providing a close-up view of plantation procedures; fruits, flowers and trees of interest ring the crater. The land belongs to Lihue Plantation and permission for this hike should be requested from their office at 2970 Kele Street (beside the Post Office), Lihu'e. Park at the base of the private road next to the Halenānahu Reservoir, about two and a half miles west of Puhi.

About three miles upstream from the ocean on the South Fork of the Wailua River, **Wailua Falls** plunge eighty feet to a pool below. This is a twin waterfall, but it is not for this reason that the river is called Wailua [two waters]; the river itself has two main branches—the North and South Forks—which merge about a mile from the sea. From the lookout point beside the falls, a steep trail descends the cliff just south of the guardrail. This trail (.5 mile) is strenuous at the best of times and after rain can be slippery and dangerous. Several short trails lead from the end of the road to the stream above the falls.

Behind Wailua, **Nounou Ridge**, known as the **Sleeping Giant**, can be climbed from either side. The trail on the *mauka* side (2 miles) climbs 1250 feet, the shorter *makai* side trail (1.5 mile) about 1000; the two run together around half a mile from the shelter at the end. Another half mile of fairly scary walking and crawling across short, narrow ridges brings you to the giant's chin and his forehead. The *mauka* trail runs off Kāmala Road (581), which is up the hill behind Coco Palms Resort,

off Kuamo'o Road (580); the *makai* trail is about a mile or so up Hale'īlio Road, which runs *mauka* off Kūhiō Highway (56) just north of Coco Palms. In both cases, the trailheads are clearly marked.

Following Kuamo'o Road (580) *mauka* for about two and a half miles past 'Ōpaeka'a Falls to the University of Hawai'i Experimental Station brings you to an unpaved road leading to the **Keāhua Arboretum**. A pamphlet available from a box on the site guides a walk (.5 mile) around the Division of Forestry project, giving details of the plants to be seen there. Across the stream, a sign marks the trailhead for the **Kuilau Ridge Trail** (2 miles) which snakes upward, affording beautiful views and, along a twisting stretch between two picnic shelters, past several small waterfalls before joining the Moalepe Trail.

The **Moalepe Trail** begins at the junction of Waipouli Road and 'Olohena Road, which can be reached from Wailua via Kuamo'o Road (580), Kāmala Road (581) to 'Olohena Road, or from Kapa'a via 'Olohena Road (581) off Kūhiō Highway (56) just south of Kapa'a Beach Park. This trail (2.5 miles) at first crosses open country then enters forest and climbs into the Makaleha Mountain Range, being joined by the Kuilau Ridge Trail about half a mile before the lookout point at the end which offers a spectacular panorama.

The most famous and most popular hike on Kaua'i is the **Kalalau Trail** (11 miles). That path through the wilderness begins at the end of Kūhiō Highway (56) on the island's North Shore and crosses several small and a couple of larger valleys at the eastern end of the Nā Pali Coast, ending in the spectacular

Kalalau Valley. Built centuries ago by the Hawaiians who once inhabited and cultivated these valleys, the trail still provides the only access to the hanging valleys and the only land access to Hanakāpī'ai and Kalalau, which also have beachheads. In addition to the main trail, described in SIGHTSEEING, about fifteen miles worth of side trails lead into the large valleys—Hanakāpī'ai, Hanakoa and Kalalau—which have pools and waterfalls galore to reward the efforts of determined hikers. Though the first couple of miles of the main trail (to Hanakāpī'ai Beach) are not all that difficult, virtually all the hiking available after that is on the strenuous side. Any destination farther in than Hanakāpī'ai requires an overnight stay unless you are dropped off by Zodiac at Kalalau Beach early in the morning and hike back out; if you choose this option, keep in mind that the view is very different depending on which way you're facing, so look back often. People exploring these wilderness areas should exercise extra caution as no emergency aid is nearby, and should also be aware that, though it is discouraged by the authorities, nudity is common and should not come as a shock to those hikers with more traditional views of propriety.

An extraordinarily complete range of backpacking and camping equipment and advice is available from **Hanalei Camping & Backpacking** (826-6664) in Hanalei's Ching Young Village. Camping is discussed under ACCOMMODATION.

There are also several interesting short treks that are better described as walks than hikes. Just past the Hanalei Bridge, straight ahead along the riverbank as you come over the bridge heading upstream, a trail into the **Hanalei Valley** (1 mile) follows the river past taro fields, fruit trees, flowers and thickets of bamboo.

Just east of the Coast Guard Station at the end of Pe'e Road in Po'ipū, a walk along the beach brings you to the site of some ancient petroglyphs, though these are at times covered with sand. Walking past the end of the road and toward the cliffs at Polihale State Park, you might be able to find the sites of Polihale Heiau and the sacred spring, and at Wailua, you can walk from Lydgate around the river mouth—passing more, similarly sand-shrouded petroglyphs—to the bridge and, crossing the bridge, up the other bank to reach Holoholokū Heiau.

KITE FLYING

Ancient Hawaiians enjoyed flying kites made of tapa or finely woven sail matting that were six or seven feet wide and up to fifteen feet long. Kaua'i's beaches are terrific and popular places for flying kites. If you didn't bring yours and want to join the fun, stop into **Hawaiian Kite Co** (742-1220) in Old Koloa Town, **High As A Kite** (822-9083) at Coconut Plantation Marketplace, or **Kauai Kite & Hobby Company** (826-9144) in Hanalei. You won't find an ancient Hawaiian model, but there are some fabulous modern creations around, mostly in brightly-colored nylon. The shapes are amazing and these

Hanakāpī'ai Beach and the Kalalau Trail continuing above it.

things really fly. Free lessons are available with purchases, and your dealer can tell you where and when demonstrations and contests are being held, in case you want to lie back on a beach mat and gaze at the sky while other people do the legwork.

FITNESS CENTERS

Jogging and running, aerobics and fully-equipped gyms are popular on Kaua'i, as elsewhere. The **Poipu Beach Fitness Center** (742-9391) at the Waiohai Resort, free to guests, is also open to the public and offers aerobics classes, and several varieties of massage in addition to fully-equipped weight and workout rooms with the latest in computerized equipment, steam, sauna and whirlpool.

The **Kauai Athletic Club** (245-5381), located at Līhu'e's Kukui Grove Center, has the full range of weights, Nautilus machines and other standard gym equipment, a swimming pool and Jacuzzi, racquetball courts, steam rooms and saunas.

The **Hanalei Athletic Club** (826-7333), located in the clubhouse of the Princeville Resort, is smaller, but has the same sort of facilities.

ENTERTAINMENT

Kaua'i's nightlife
Lu'au
Hawaiian music
Calendar of events

ENTERTAINMENT and NIGHTLIFE

The idyllic rural environment of Kaua'i affords a limited supply of entertainment and nightlife, but more and more restaurant and hotel lounges are providing live music regularly, particularly during the after-dinner hours. A Polynesian show or a lu'au is on almost every first-time visitor's agenda, and most seek out Hawaiian music, knowing they're not likely to find it anywhere else.

This section outlines the entertainment scene generally. Specifics change often, and details are available from free tourist publications (many listing only advertisers) and from local newspapers, magazines and radio stations. Reliable sources include the weekly Garden Island Calendar in the Sunday edition of *The Garden Island* newspaper, and the semiannual *Kaua'i Magazine*'s Upcoming Celebrations section; this colorful magazine also presents interesting articles on local places, people and events.

POLYNESIAN SHOWS

On nearly every island in the Pacific Ocean, Polynesian or not, the 'Polynesian Show' has become virtually *de rigueur* tourist entertainment. These shows stage performances based on the traditional music, dance and costumes of Hawai'i, Tahiti, Sāmoa, New Zealand and, occasionally, Tonga and the Cook Islands; sometimes, primarily Melanesian Fiji is also included.

Available on Kaua'i at all lu'au, at shopping center stages, and as a dinner show at the Kauai Resort Hotel, these spectacles are glitzy, show-biz interpretations, and the Tahitian *tamure* almost invariably highlights the evening with its fast-paced hip-swiveling, grass skirts, tall headdresses and wildly beating drums. Another show-stopper is the Samoan fire dance or its close kin, the knife dance. Hawaiian hula is usually the *'auana*, or modern, variety, though some shows include a traditional *'ōlapa* or *kahiko* hula as well. The Maori (New Zealand) contributions are always a *poi* dance (*poi* in Maori is the white balls on string that the women manipulate so expertly in some of their dances), and the fierce *haka* where men challenge each other (and their audience) with spears and protruding tongues.

LU'AU

Undoubtedly the lu'au is the most famous feast on your entertainment menu. This highly-civilized Polynesian custom resembles the American Thanksgiving feast, except that the lu'au can be given at any time, for any reason. One good, traditional reason for a lu'au is to honor and entertain visitors, so your attendance at one is entirely appropriate. The feast is named after the taro tops [*lū'au*] that are always served at one. Cooked with coconut cream, they are delectably delicious and unreservedly recommended. Other traditional fare on such occasions includes such dishes as *laulau*, small packages of fish, pork, chicken or beef, with taro tops, wrapped in ti or banana leaves and baked; *poi*, a thick, purplish paste made from the cooked and pounded base of the taro plant (the staple starch food of the Hawaiians); *kālua* pig, traditionally cooked in an underground oven [*imu*]; and *haupia*, thick, creamy coconut pudding. The introduction of European and Asian foods to Hawai'i has added great variety to the culinary concoctions that are now traditional at a lu'au. There is so much to choose from that the lu'au can please the palate of almost everyone.

Though the focus of this feast is food, a lu'au includes a host of entertainments to feast the eye and ear as well. Music, dance, and usually a bit of comedy enhance the festive atmosphere and add to the fun. They are staged on a grand scale. Prices at the different venues are comparable, except at Tahiti Nui, which is a lot less expensive.

The closest thing you'll find to a private, family lu'au is the one held on Monday, Wednesday and Friday at **Tahiti Nui** in Hanalei (826-6277). Hosted by Tahitian matriarch Louise Marston, the evening's entertainment features hula of ancient Kaua'i by Hālau o Hanalei and includes dances from Tahiti; this feast is often enlivened by local musicians who just happen by. A really special show is that by the Punua family and their Hula Hālau o Ku'ulei Punua, accompanying the lu'au at the **Sheraton Coconut Beach** in Kapa'a (822-3455), held nightly except Monday in their special longhouse. The **Kauai Resort Hotel** at Wailua (245-3931) presents a garden lu'au every night except Monday and Saturday, and the **Sheraton-Kauai** at Po'ipū (742-1661) a showroom lu'au on Sunday and Wednesday, the latter featuring mostly Tahitian dancing and Hawaiian music. The nightly **Smith's Tropical Paradise Luau**, at the gardens of the same name in Wailua (822-4654), includes a stage extravaganza in the outdoor Lagoon Theater, complete with volcanic eruption and greetings from Pele. In addition to the Polynesian dances already mentioned, this show includes dances from China, Japan and the Philippines, major contributors to Hawai'i's ethnic soup. This lively and interesting show, produced by Kenny and Carol Casil, is worth a peek, even if you have seen 'Polynesian shows' before. If you want to attend a show only, this option is available at all venues.

DINNER SHOWS

Though all dinner shows have some Polynesian content and a distinctive 'island' touch, not all dinner shows are 'Polynesian shows'. Except for the lu'au, there are not many on Kaua'i.

The nightly **Larry Rivera Show** at the **Coco Palms Resort** is primarily a Hawaiian show. The **Kauai Resort Hotel** has a nightly Polynesian dinner show in addition to its lu'au show, and also brings entertainers from O'ahu and occasionally from other islands and elsewhere for limited weekend showroom engagements.

The Westin Kauai's **Royal Boathouse Supper Club** features a

Hawaiian dinner show nightly except Monday. The restaurant **Club Jetty** (245-4970), a local institution, has a nightly show, usually performed by family and friends. All have a late, after-dinner 'cocktail' seating, which is significantly less expensive.

HULA

The hula is the heartbeat of Hawai'i. An integral part of the ritual life of the ancients, the old hula never died. New dances derived from it became popular entertainment for visiting sailors, who paid well to witness these alterations, but Hawaiians didn't fundamentally connect this new and lucrative enterprise with their sacred dance. Reviled by missionaries as 'obscene', the old dance was taken underground and taught in secret, while the new dance thrived in places where religious reformers held no sway. Thus there developed two distinct classes of hula, the ancient and the modern.

Hula 'ōlapa, more recently known as *hula kahiko*, the old style, is performed to the accompaniment of chanting and percussion *only*. Traditionally, the dance was done to accompany the chant, which was of primary importance, and it was performed on most occasions by men. Though most hula groups today have a preponderance of women, the men's hula is every bit as beautiful, and is energetic with a virile grace that seems absent from the aggressive men's dances of other Polynesian cultures. Chanting, too, is an art that is experiencing a revival, along with the upsurge of interest in the Hawaiian language, which is always used in the chants. The women's hula is softer than the men's, but still has strength and precision. Precision is a vital element of this hula style, and while there is ample scope for the enactment of modern tales in the ancient mode, the rules are strict and strictly followed. There were, though, and still are distinctive hula styles, and Kaua'i's hula has special features—such as treadleboard percussion—that are primarily associated with that island.

It is interesting to note that the most famous symbol of the hula, indeed of Hawai'i—the grass skirt—is not Hawaiian at all. The grass skirt was introduced from Micronesia by laborers from the Gilbert Islands in the early nineteenth century. Hawaiians subsequently used native materials, such as ti leaves, in a similar fashion but they were always fresh and green out of respect for the gods, a strictly Hawaiian innovation. Prior to European visitations, their garments had been of barkcloth [*kapa*]. During the reign of King Kalākaua, when by royal decree the hula was again performed in public, the European clothing of the time was worn in the dance, and hula from that era are still performed in costumes of the period. *Hula ku'i*, a transitional form that combines traditional hula movements with those of nineteenth-century European ballroom dance, arose at this time. Prior to this innovation, men and women seldom danced together; in most ancient hula performed today, they still do not.

Hula 'auana, the modern style, is much more flexible than its ancient forebear, just as modern ballet can be interpreted more freely than classical. Its costuming is limited only by the imagination and is keyed to the story being told. Modern hula is usually accompanied by both melody and lyrics as well as ukuleles, guitars and other instruments, and the songs may be in any language, though English and Hawaiian are most common. There are many *hālau* [hula schools], but their performances are not regularly scheduled. It's well worth scanning the local papers for *ho'olaule'a* or other community events (also see CALENDAR OF EVENTS) that feature hula, because what you see can be significantly different from what you see in a Polynesian show, especially if you catch a good *kahiko*. Some of the Kaua'i *hālau* that cannot be seen in commercial performances are: **Hula Hālau o Keao**, which does only *hula 'ōlapa*, **Ka 'Imi Na'auao o Hawai'i Nei, Nakaholokua, Hālau Kanikapahu o Lohia'u**, and **Nā Hula o Kaohikukapulani Atooi Marama**, which includes Tahitian dances. Amongst the most appealing sights you'll see is a well-trained hula troupe of children [*keiki*]. Notable Kaua'i *keiki* groups are **Hālau o Kala'au'ale** and **Hula Hui o Kapunahala.**

HAWAIIAN MUSIC

Though neither melody nor harmony had existed in Polynesian tradition prior to European contact, the peoples of the Islands demonstrated remarkable natural affinity with and talent for both. They also adopted enthusiastically the stringed instruments these visitors introduced, and each Polynesian group has developed a distinctive musical style during the past century or two.

The guitar is probably the instrument most commonly used by Hawaiian musicians today, but its baby brother, the ukulele, is most strongly identified with Hawai'i. *'Ukulele* is, in fact, a Hawaiian word. It means 'leaping flea' and was first applied as a nickname to Edward Purvis, a popular nineteenth century player of the instrument who jumped around while he strummed. Brought to Hawai'i by Portuguese laborers in 1879, the diminutive instrument was known to them as *braquinho*. The other stringed instrument immutably linked with Hawai'i is the steel guitar, played horizontally with a metal slide. Last but certainly not least is the distinctively Hawaiian 'slack key' guitar, a tuning effect achieved by loosening the strings.

Today's island music has continued to evolve and is now less stereotypical and more grounded in true expression of the feelings of island life. Within it, naturally, are varieties—and insertions from the contemporary idiom—but the unique island flavor is discernible throughout.

In addition to the Dinner Shows described above, a few venues regularly present Hawaiian music. The Sheraton Princeville hosts small groups of Hawaiian musicians nightly at the **Lime Tree** lobby lounge. **The Lagoon Bar** at Coco Palms Resort features mixed Hawaiian and contemporary music in the early evening. The Sheraton Coconut Beach has live music in its

Cook's Landing lounge, and the Sheraton-Kauai in its Drum Lounge. From mid-afternoon through early evening, contemporary Hawaiian music is played at the Verandah Bar, fronting Kalapakī Beach at the Westin Kauai. The Kauai Hilton features live Hawaiian music in its Lobby Lounge in the very early evening. Tahiti Nui (826-6277) presents local groups playing Hawaiian or country and western music. The Rib 'n Tail restaurant and lounge (822-9632) presents varying musical styles and sometimes hosts visiting performers from Honolulu, as does Interlude (335-3144) in Hanapēpē.

LOCAL MUSICIANS

Some of Kaua'i's most notable and popular entertainers are listed here in alphabetical order. With a few exceptions, they rarely play the same venue for long; free tourist newspapers such as the Kauai Beach Press are good sources of information on who's playing where. Popular Hawaiian recording artists are listed in The Essential Guide to O'ahu.

Glen A'una heads a trio playing and singing a mix of old and new Hawaiian tunes. The Frankie K Trio sings and plays a range of Hawaiian and contemporary music. Nalani Goaez is the only local stand-up comic presently performing regularly on Kaua'i; he can sing, too. Ipo Kahaunaele & Friends is a trio playing mostly traditional Hawaiian music, but also Hawaiian contemporary. The Kahelelani Serenaders, from the island of Ni'ihau, sing popular Hawaiian favorites.

A local family trio, Ke Ānuenue Serenaders play mostly Hawaiian music along with some contemporary tunes. Koko Kaneali'i sings and plays guitar and autoharp. The Kaua'i Boys play Hawaiian contemporary music. Hal Kinnaman plays exquisite classical and slack key guitar. Local male trio Mālie presents their own original Hawaiian music along with traditional favorites.

CONTEMPORARY and ROCK

A few places present live contemporary music, which often gets louder as the hour gets later. Some of the softer sounds can be heard at the Sheraton Coconut Beach's Cook's Landing, a mixture of Hawaiian and contemporary musical fare, at the Poipu Beach Club at the Poipu Beach Hotel, and at the Hanalei Bay Resort's Happy Talk Lounge. Cafe Mokihana (245-8999) in Līhu'e offers mixed Hawaiian and contemporary music on Friday and Saturday nights, and The Lagoon Bar at Coco Palms Resort features soft Hawaiian and contemporary music in the early evening and dance music when the dinner show in the adjacent Lagoon Dining Room is over. I'ulani Isle (826-7680) at Princeville Center hosts nightly live music. Weekend daytime shows are a regular feature at Kukui Grove Shopping Center.

Louder shows include the country rock at the Jolly Roger (822-3451) in the Coconut Plantation Marketplace, and the rhythms throb into the late hours for after-dinner patrons at **Club Jetty** (245-4970).

Kaua'i has three 'disco' dance clubs, featuring recorded music. **Gilligan's** at the Kauai Hilton, plays loud, hard-hitting rock. **Ukiyo** at the Sheraton Princeville, exquisitely decorated in Japanese warrior style, starts the evening with light rock, generally getting heavier and louder as the night wears on, but the disc jockey gears his selections to the audience on hand. The Westin Kauai's **Paddling Club** bills itself as a five-level, high energy, adult entertainment venue.

JAZZ and PIANO BARS

Soft jazz music is featured, on Sundays only, at the Hanalei Bay Resort's **Happy Talk Lounge.**

Low-key piano bar entertainment is offered at the Waiohai Hotel's **Tamarind Lounge**, next to their 5☆ restaurant of the same name, and in the lounge of the classy **Inn on the Cliffs**, at the Westin Kauai.

Piano with stand-up bass is featured at the Westin's **Colonnade Bar.**

VISITING ARTISTS

Occasionally, musicians from the US mainland perform on Kaua'i, but visiting artists are more likely from Honolulu. The venue of choice for most of these special events is the Kaua'i War Memorial Convention Hall in Līhu'e, as it is the only large auditorium on the island. The **Kauai Resort Hotel** in Wailua regularly hosts visiting Hawaiian entertainers, who occasionally perform also at the **Rib 'n Tail** in Kapa'a (822-9632) and **Interlude** in Hanapēpē (335-3144).

SOCIAL DRINKING

After a hectic day of sightseeing or sand-snoozing, many people just want to relax with a drink. These lounges are quiet enough for conversation. Soft sounds of Hawaiian music provide a pleasant background at the **Lime Tree Lounge** in the lobby of the Sheraton Princeville. Though seating is very limited, the terrace outside **Ukiyo**, the dance club at the Sheraton Princeville, is a great place to watch the sun set, as this spot overlooking Hanalei Bay has one of the best views in the world. A similar view is available at the **Happy Talk Lounge** at the Hanalei Bay Resort.

Tahiti Nui (826-6277) in Hanalei is quiet enough for conversation only until the live music begins. **The Lagoon Bar** at Coco Palms Resort overlooks that famous lagoon and provides soft music until the show in the adjacent Lagoon Dining Room begins. The Kauai Hilton's **Lobby Bar** is a quiet, pleasant, open place for early evening cocktails. The Sheraton Coconut Beach's **Cook's Landing** overlooks the hotel garden and provides soft, live music. The **Drum Lounge** at the Sheraton-Kauai in Po'ipū is also a great sunset location and is quiet until the live music starts. Also in

Po'ipū the lounge at the **Beach House Restaurant** (742-7575) is a quiet nook with a great westward ocean view.

All the contemporary/rock dance venues fall into the 'too loud to talk' category. Once the live music starts at **Tahiti Nui** (826-6277), the small size of the lounge combined with the volume of the sound makes conversation a strain.

The larger room at **I'ulani Isle** (826-7680) affords a greater degree of choice for the listener, loudness depending somewhat on where you sit as well as on who's playing. The late evening dance session at Coco Palms Resort's **Lagoon Bar** is a trifle on the voluble side, and **Jolly Roger** (822-3451) can get a little raucous in the late hours, as can **Club Jetty** (245-4970).

THEATRE

The **Kauai Community Players** is a very active and talented amateur theatrical group which offers an almost continuous program of varying musical and dramatic plays throughout the year. Performances are generally held at the Parish Hall of the Congregational Church on Nāwiliwili Road in Līhu'e, opposite Kukui Grove Center, on Thursday, Friday and Saturday nights. Check the local newspapers or *Kaua'i Magazine* for the current production.

CINEMA

Films currently popular on the US mainland play at the local cinemas, which are located in Līhu'e at Kukui Grove Center (245-5055), in Kapa'a at Coconut Plantation Marketplace (822-9391), and in Kīlauea (828-1722). Check the local newspaper for current program listings.

Kaua'i also gets a scaled-down version of the **Hawaii International Film Festival**, a major annual showing of films from Asian and Pacific nations sponsored each autumn by the East-West Center in Honolulu.

CALENDAR OF EVENTS

FEBRUARY

Captain Cook Celebration—Waimea Town party with refreshments, lu'au, parade, entertainment, dancing, canoe race, re-enactment of Captain Cook landing, 10km foot race and bicycle race. Waimea Mainstreet Project 338-1226

LPGA Women's Kemper Open Golf Tournament—Helene Curtis ProAm in a free, week-long event, last two days televised. Princeville 826-3580 (Feb-March)

MARCH

Prince Kuhio Festival—pageantry, songs and dances from the era of Prince Kūhiō. Canoe races at Wailua Beach and a royal ball. Līhu'e 245-3971

Prince Kuhio Rodeo—islandwide event with food and fun for a small fee. Pooku Stables, Princeville 826-6777

APRIL

Buddha Day—at Island temples statewide; celebrates the birth of Buddha. Hawaii Buddhist Council 538-3805 (Honolulu)

MAY

May Day is Lei Day in Hawai'i—islandwide annual lei-making competition, May 1. Kaua'i Museum, Līhu'e 245-6931

May Day by the Bay—a Lei Day celebration. Crafts and ethnic food booths. Princeville 826-6591

JUNE

King Kamehameha Celebration—State holiday honoring Kamehameha the Great, Hawai'i's first monarch. Kaua'i Island—Parade from Vidinha Stadium to County Building; ho'olaule'a and arts and crafts at finish of parade. Līhu'e State Council for Hawaiian Heritage 536-6540 (Honolulu)

JULY

Kekaha 4th of July Celebration—a small-town fun affair with carnival, parade, food booths, *keiki* contests and more put on by the Kekaha Community Association. Kekaha 245-8311

King Kong Ultra Triathlon—a 2-mile swim, 90-mile bike ride, 18-mile run in Kaua'i's wilderness. Benefit for Gorilla Foundation. Hanalei 826-9343

AUGUST

Pooku Annual Hanalei Stampede—a statewide rodeo held at Pooku Stables; includes bronc and bull riding, food, music and dancing. Princeville 826-6777

Garden Island Half Marathon and 5km, 10km Runs—starts at Sheraton Coconut Beach Hotel, Kapa'a. 245-7255

West Kauai Summer Festival—old-fashioned end-of-summer beach party; games, races, Hawaiian crafts, lu'au and cookout, beauty pageant, hula, street dancing and a concert. Waimea Mainstreet Project 338-1226

SEPTEMBER

Kaua'i County Fair—exhibits, produce, flowers, 4-H and commercial livestock, E.K. Fernandez rides and games, food and entertainment. Labor Day weekend, Thursday to Sunday. Kaua'i War Memorial Convention Hall, Līhu'e 245-4471

Aloha Week Festivals—Hawaiian pageantry, parades, *ho'olaule'a*, canoe races, and a variety of entertainment and stage shows. 245-3385

OCTOBER

Kauai Loves You Triathlon—a world championship (Low Distance) super series event; about a 1-mile swim, 40-mile bike ride and 7-mile run. Begins and ends at Hanalei Pier. 826-9232

DECEMBER

Hawaii International Film Festival—Kaua'i portion is scaled-down version of East-West Center Honolulu event; week-long showings of about twenty feature films and documentaries; opening cocktail party introduces film directors, producers, actors, Kaua'i dignitaries; Aloha Awards Banquet to close festival. Kauai Hilton 245-1955

Bodhi Day—Buddhist temples comemmorate 'Day of Enlightenment'. Hawaii Buddhist Council 538-3805 (Honolulu), Lihue Hongwanji 245-6262

Christmas in Waimea—Christmas parade from Waimea High School to Hofgaard Park, candlelight tour of missions and churches, caroling in the streets, arrival of Santa Claus, displays of 'Twelve Days of Christmas—Hawaiian-Style'. Waimea Mainstreet Project 338-1226

SHOPPING

Centers
Aloha wear
Art
Handcrafts

SHOPPING

Most of Kaua'i's visitors go shopping—for *something*—during their island holiday This categorized listing points out some of the more notable shops. Addresses and telephone numbers of these are listed at the back of this book as an appendix.

CENTERS

There are numerous shopping centers on Kaua'i; the big ones have a good cross section of shops and services, and many offer late night shopping. **Old Koloa Town**, at the end of the famous Tunnel of Trees, is a delightful modern rendition of the old town center, the buildings having been renovated and the area revitalized. It's a pleasant setting for the wide variety of shops that have congregated here and at night is lit up like a ship in port with strings of zillions of tiny white lights. Businesses include sport and tour companies as well as clothing, jewelry, art, flowers and photo needs, and several restaurants and snack shops. A jitney service shuttles shoppers around the town. **Kiahuna Shopping Village**, located opposite Kiahuna Plantation Resort on Po'ipū Road, is a slick, modern complex with upbeat shops selling clothing, jewelry, fine art and gifts. It also houses restaurants and snack shops.

Kilohana in Puhi is part historic house museum and part shopping center, offering arts and crafts, clothing, jewelry and gifts as well as a plant shop, a snack shop and two restaurants. Carriage rides around the grounds of this former plantation estate are narrated, giving the history of the family that owns it.

Kukui Grove Center in Līhu'e is a large, modern center, with three department stores—Liberty House, Sears and JC Penney—a drugstore, supermarket, fifteen eateries and two dozen small shops plus a health club, a cinema and banking and professional services. This center also has an outdoor stage where performances are irregularly held.

Rice Shopping Center in the heart of Līhu'e offers clothing and fabrics. **Kinipopo** in Kapa'a and **Waipouli Plaza**, on Kūhiō Highway in Waipouli have a small range of shops and restaurants.

The Market Place at Coconut Plantation, commonly referred to as 'Coconut Plantation Marketplace' or even simply 'Coconut Plantation', in Kapa'a is big, modern and beautiful with more than seventy shops and boutiques, selling clothing, jewelry, island gifts, handcrafts and fine art, plus two cinemas and several restaurants, lounges and snack bars. It, too, has an outdoor stage where a Polynesian 'photo-show' is held every Thurdsay, Friday and Saturday at 4pm.

Princeville Center has a large supermarket, bank and service station and a wide range of small shops and services including clothing, jewelry, photo supplies, restaurants, flowers, kites, sports equipment sales and rental, ice cream and desserts.

Ching Young Village in Hanalei has the full range of food stores and restaurants, clothing, souvenir and variety stores, arts and crafts, bank, outdoor equipment rentals and tour companies, and a small museum. It also has an outdoor stage where performances are held irregularly.

ALOHA WEAR

Aloha shirts, in bright, flowery prints, and *mu'umu'us* [long, loose dresses] put visitors in the light-hearted 'aloha' spirit quicker than a mai-tai. People in Kaua'i really do wear these casual, comfortable clothes, although couples with matching outfits are usually found only onstage.

The well-known **Hilo Hattie's**, **Happy Kauaian** and **Tahiti Imports** have shops at Coconut Plantation with resort wear for the whole family; the latter also has locations at the Sheraton Coconut Beach and Sheraton-Kauai Hotels and at the Wailua Marina. The **Kapaia Stitchery** in Kapaia, at the edge of Līhu'e, carries island fashions for men and women. **Rainbow Rags**, a manufacturer's outlet store, is in the Rice Shopping Center.

Vicky's Fabric Shop in Kapa'a offers custom-made aloha wear and, for something uncommon, **Lina's Fashions & Fabrics** in Rice Shopping Center offers appliqued mu'umu'us.

Marta's Boat in Kapa'a presents children's island fashions, made and sold by the delightful Marta. Also specializing in kids' clothes are **Tutu's Hale Keiki** at Coconut Plantation and **Tutu's Kiddy Korner** at Kilohana in Puhi.

DEPARTMENT STORES

Hawai'i's home-grown department stores are **Liberty House** (Kukui Grove Center, Coconut Plantation, The Waiohai Resort) and **McInerny's** (Coconut Plantation Marketplace), and they carry the latest fashions in an atmosphere comparable to that of US mainland stores. **JC Penney** and **Sears**, both located at the Kukui Grove Center, differ little from their Mainland branches except that they have aloha wear and Hawaiian souvenir departments.

T-SHIRTS

Everyone wears T-shirts. Their popularity never seems to fade, and their diversity has unfolded in almost miraculous permutations over the past few years. Fortunes have been made.

The classic success story and the undisputed king of trendy tees in Hawai'i is **Crazy Shirts**, located in Coconut Plantation, Kiahuna Shopping Village and Old Koloa Town. Their shops carry a large selection of designs, but few styles. Their hallmark is the delightful device of depicting on the back of the shirt a rear view of whatever is on the front.

Spinning Dolphin Designs at

SHOPPING

Ching Young Village has solved the problem of not having in stock the right design in the right size, style and color; they screen the designs you choose onto the garments you choose—T-shirts, T-dresses and sweatshsirts—on the spot, while you wait.

WOMEN'S BOUTIQUES

The **Kong Lung Co.** in Kīlauea presents an exceptionally fine selection of tropical clothing and a large variety of silks. **Cane Field Clothing Company** at Kilohana offers both evening and casual wear, and **See You in China** at Kukui Grove Center has a good selection of the out-of-the-ordinary.

Kauai Bay Cargo Company in Ching Young Village and in Kapa'a offers a delightful and uncommon selection of lightweight casual and semi-casual clothing in soft colors, prints and solids. **Reyn's**, famous for fine quality fashions with the fabric turned inside out, has a shop at Coconut Plantation.

Andrade & Company sells contemporary fashions at Coconut Plantation, the Sheraton Princeville and the Sheraton-Kauai. **The Kauai Queen** in Kalāheo specializes in large sizes.

MEN'S STORES

Koloa Men in Kōloa is a men's specialty store. The men's department at **Kong Lung Co.** in Kīlauea has a fine selection of tropical and safari clothing and aloha wear. **Reyn's** at Coconut Plantation has a great selection of inside-out aloha shirts, and these are also available at the **Princeville Plantation Store** at Princeville Center. **Shanora of Kauai** at Ching Young Village offers custom-made fashions, and **Andrade & Company** sells the latest in contemporary men's fashions.

SWIMWEAR

Kaua'i's selection of swimwear is outstanding. Swimwear specialists are **That Tropical Feeling** and **Swim Inn** in Old Koloa Town. **Toucans** at Princeville Center and at Kinipopo Shopping Village has a large selection of swimwear in addition to other casual fashions. **Kerrysma** in Kapa'a also carries a range of swimwear and contemporary clothing. **Koloa Casuals & Ocean Sports** features swimming apparel and other beachwear and casual clothing.

FABRIC

Those who prefer to craft their own tropical fashions can find printed fabrics in shops such as **The Kapaia Stitchery** in Kapaia near Lihu'e, **Plantation Stitchery** at Coconut Plantation, **Vicky's Fabric Shop** in Kapa'a and **Lina's Fashions & Fabrics** in Rice Shopping

Center. The unique screen-printed fabric used in the fashions at **Tahiti** **Imports** is also available by the yard.

LEATHER GOODS

Lee Sands at the Hawaiian Trading Post in Lāwaʻi on the corner of Kaumualiʻi Highway (50) and Kōloa Road, has a wide range of accessories—including some jewelry—made from an astonishing array of exotic skins including eelskin, sharkskin, sea snake, salmon, lizard, mink and chicken feet!

Eelskin can also be found at a number of other Kauaʻi merchants.

JEWELRY

In Hawaiʻi, leis of tiny shells from Niʻihau have long been treasured heirlooms. On Kauaʻi, almost all jewelry and gift stores carry necklaces [*lei*], bracelets [*kūpeʻe*] and earrings of Niʻihau shells, the only shell classified as a gem and insurable. Difficult to see in their natural environment, these tiny, varicolored shells are found only on the tiny island of Niʻihau and on the southwest coast of Kauaʻi. Multiple strands fetch very high prices. The smaller *kahelelani* shells are the most expensive. There is a daily market of outdoor stalls in the park next to the Spouting Horn in Poʻipū where prices are lower, but you will not find the highest quality here either.

Kauaʻi also has some fine jewelers making custom creations— such as **Jim Saylor Jewelers** and **The Goldsmith's Gallery** in Kapaʻa. Natural quartz jewelry, raw crystals and gemstones are the specialty of **A Crystal Journey** at Kilohana. Coral is featured by **Coral Grotto** at Kukui Grove Center and by **Coral House of Kauai** at Menehune Shopping Village. Fine shell, jade and other jewelry is available at **Kong Lung Co.** in Kīlauea, including unusual creations like jewelry made from twisted silk. **Koloa Gold** in Old Koloa Town has netsuke as well as fine jewels, and Coconut Plantation has no less than nine jewelry stores. Many jewelers feature Hawaiian 'heirloom' jewelry—heavy bracelets and rings in gold with names enameled in black Victorian-style lettering. These are sometimes offered as transliterations into Hawaiian. You might like knowing what the word that sounds like your name actually means; check a good Hawaiian dictionary, or the book *Hawaiian Names*, by Eileen Root.

ART

Kauaʻi's tranquil tropical environment attracts artists of every ilk. One of the island's outstanding artists is **Laka Morton**, whose brooding portraits of Hawaiians have dramatic appeal. Hawaiian seascape master **Roy Tabora** paints as though he has light in his brush.

Himself a resident of O'ahu, Tabora's sole agent is Kaua'i's **Kahn Galleries**, with locations at the Sheraton Princeville and Coconut Plantation; this gallery also features a few other select artists, such as **Robert Lyn Nelson**, famous for his undersea paintings with the landscape above. Nelson's work can also be found at **Port of Kauai** in Coconut Plantation and at **The Ship Store Gallery** in Kiahuna Shopping Village, which specializes in nautical art and antiques. The **Lighthouse Gallery**, on Lighthouse Road behind Kong Lung in Kīlauea, carries an excellent range of large and small paintings, prints, sculpture and other works—almost all by local artists—and offers custom framing. **Stones Gallery**, with locations at Kukui Grove Center and Kilohana offers a similar range of primarily local paintings, prints, posters, crafts and custom framing. Also at Kilohana, **Kilohana Galleries** sells paintings, prints, ceramics and gifts. A similar range of creations by local artists is available at **Artisans' Guild of Kauai** in Hanalei's Ching Young Village. At

Princeville Center, **Princeville Galleries** offers a good selection of fine art, and in Old Koloa Town, **Kahana Kii Gallery of Koloa** has shell leis, handcrafts, sculpture and ceramics as well as local art. The **James Hoyle Gallery** and **The Art Shop** in Līhu'e sell the pink and purple land- and seascapes of local painter James Hoyle.

The **Island Heritage Collection** art shops in Old Koloa Town and Kapa'a feature signed, limited edition lithographs of well-known local or part-time resident artists who specialize in Hawaiian subject matter. The list includes **Anthony Casay**, a split-view land- and seascape artist; **Leslie B. DeMille**, an oil and pastel portraitist and two-month-a-year resident of Maui for the past twenty years; Big Island resident and realist **Mary Koski**; **Luigi Fumigalli**, whose Hawaiian and Japanese women are rendered with intense color; **Kristin Zambucka**, capturing the tranquil strength of Polynesian men and women in soft pastels; and **Les Nitta**, whose hallmark is airbrush floral painting.

HANDCRAFTS

Hawaiians traditionally wove and plaited the leaves of *hala*, or pandanus [*lauhala*] into all manner of useful items including floormats and baskets; today the range has been expanded to include handbags, lampshades, placemats and much more. Similar items are made in tapa (barkcloth), but this is not, alas, the traditional Hawaiian *kapa*, as the art of making the fine felt-like material the Hawaiians produced—the finest in all Polynesia—was lost generations ago. The tapa you buy

here is, however, authentic; it is produced by hand using the ancient methods in Sāmoa, Tonga and Fiji.

Another traditional craft still very much alive and thriving is the making of permanent leis. These were and are made from feathers, seeds and shells. Ni'ihau shell leis now command hefty prices (see Jewelry above), but attractive strands of other local shells are quite reasonably priced. Feather leis are a bit more expensive, but require much more time and care in the making as well as more material. Feather neck and head leis were traditionally worn by the *ali'i*, as were *lei niho palaoa*, hook-shaped pendants, originally made of whale ivory. Later made of wood or stone—or of walrus tusk or beef bone brought by merchant sailors— these hook-shaped pendants became so popular that virtually everyone wore them. Woodcarving, too, has expanded far beyond its traditional application in creating *akua ki'i*, images representing gods. Indigenous woods such as koa, milo and monkeypod are carved into decorative bowls and other utensils. You can also buy modern renditions of ancient gods, as well as more mundane figures such as fish and pineapples. Most of these crafts can be found at gift stores all over Kaua'i. Custom koa frames can be found at **Kauai Images** as well as at the galleries mentioned above; custom anything can be designed for you at **Woodtrends** in Keālia near Kapa'a, or you can buy one of the house specialties such as a signed and numbered heirloom rocking horse—not a traditional Hawaiian item but, done in koa, definitely a treasure for many generations.

SHOPPING

99

ANTIQUES

Fine Asian, American and European antiques are amongst the treasures at **Kong Lung Co.** in Kīlauea. **Half Moon Trading Co.** at Kilohana specializes in Japanese antiques: furniture, kimonos and folk art. **The Ship Store Gallery** is dedicated to nautical antiques and maritime art including scrimshaw, old and new. **Koloa Gold** in Old Koloa Town carries netsuke figures. **Collectibles & Fine Junque** is self-explanatory, and **The Only Show in Town** in Kapa'a bills itself as Kaua'i's largest antique and vintage clothing shop.

FRUIT, FLOWERS and FOLIAGE

Cuttings and seeds of tropical plants provide a living reminder of a colorful Hawaiian holiday and fresh fruits or flower leis make delightful gifts for friends back home. Shipping is easy to arrange; many vendors will handle this for you. Some fruits and flowers are subject to quarantine regulations imposed by the US Department of Agriculture and are prohibited from entry to Mainland states.

Pineapples are no problem (though few are grown on Kaua'i), but professional packing is preferable to ensure they arrive undam- aged. The only papayas allowed are those treated, passed and sealed by agricultural inspectors. Only the frozen flesh of mangoes is allowed; the seeds are forbidden unless they are split open and inspected. Guavas and passionfruit [*liliko'i*] are not allowed at all. Coconuts are fine and fun. Don't bother packing them; just buy them (or pick them up off the ground in an area where the trees remain untrimmed) still in the outer husk. This is excellent natural packing and has served to float coconuts for thousands of miles across open oceans to be dashed by waves, unharmed, upon foreign shores. Not only that, they survive the rough handling of the US Postal Service. Just write the address on the coconut itself—unwrapped—and paste on the postage stamps. The Post Office actually accepts these unorthodox parcels. **The Nut Cracker Sweet** ships fresh fruit; **Farm Fresh Fruit Stand** will pack fresh fruit and deliver it to the airport for your pickup at the airline check-in counter.

Be cautious when buying leis to take home. Flowers such as roses, *maunaloa* and jade, berries such as mock orange and *mokihana*, and leaves such as *hala* and *kikuyu* are prohibited and leis containing them will be confiscated. Many flower shops offer shipping service to the Mainland. **Say It With Flowers, Floratica Hawaii, Business Is Blooming, Coco Palms Florist, Flowers Forever, Flowers of the Rainbow** and others offer this service.

Sterile cuttings and seeds of many tropical and semitropical plants are sold in sealed packages that have been passed and certified by the US Department of Agriculture, and these will pass inspection without difficulty. They are sold in many souvenir-type shops and in almost all plant and garden shops.

For specific inquiries and further details you may telephone the Kaua'i office of the State of Hawai'i Department of Agriculture at 245-4413 and ask for Mainland export information. If you're leaving the country, you can take whatever you like, but there's no guarantee of its passing quarantine inspection in your country of arrival.

SOUVENIRS

The number one stops for souvenir and gift items are **Woolworth** and **Longs Drug Store** in Kukui Grove Center. Another good, inexpensive place is **Village Variety** at Ching Young Village, which carries a good selection of postcards, posters, art prints and souvenir items as well as the typical range of merchandise you'd expect to find in a variety store. **Island Camera & Gift Shops** in the Sheraton Princeville and the Coco Palms Resort carry gift items, and **Foodland** supermarkets also have souvenir sections.

More upbeat gifts and local craft items are found at nearly a hundred shops in every hotel and shopping center on the island as well as in some out-of-the-way places, like **Kauai Hidden Treasures** hidden in Kekaha, next to the Post Office near Waimea Canyon Road, **Da Latest Kine** in Waimea or **Town Store** in Hanapēpē.

SHELLS

Tropical shells are a popular souvenir item for visitors. Numerous shops carry a variety of tropical shells—in better condition than any you are likely to find on the beach if you find any—as well as an incredible potpourri of useful and decorative things made from shells.

Shells International at Coconut Plantation, **Pearly Shells** in Po'ipū,

Linda's Creation in Līhu'e and the Cowrie Shop and Nature's Gallery in Kapa'a are all shell specialists.

Sea Reflections in Kilohana Plantation also specializes in shells and sea-related items.

BOOKS

At the back of this guide, we have listed books we recommend for more detailed information on Hawai'i. Most of these are easy to find in our local bookstores, but may be not so easy to find at home. Books are the surest way to take a permanent remembrance of Hawai'i home with you. The huge Mainland chain **Waldenbooks** has shops at both Kukui Grove Center and Coconut Plantation. Their extensive Hawaiiana collection is overseen by knowledgeable, friendly staff. **Rainbow Books**, also at Kukui Grove Center, highlights Hawaiiana and guidebooks and has a good selection of bestsellers and children's books. Kauaiana in particular is the natural specialty of the shop at the **Kaua'i Museum**, which also carries a delightful range of gift items related to the Museum's areas of interest. While specializing in maps and books related to the outdoor life, the small book section at **Hanalei Camping & Backpacking** in Hanalei's Ching Young Village has an astonishing array of excellent books on all sorts of subjects, including works on other Pacific cultures. **Happy Talk Books**, also in Hanalei, at Kuahale Center, specializes in Hawaiiana paperbacks and also trades in used books.

RECORDS, TAPES and DISCS

The biggest recorded music merchant on Kaua'i is **Jack Wada Electronics** in Līhu'e. Another place to buy records is **Gem** in the Lihue Shopping Center, at the junction of the Kūhiō (56) and Kaumuali'i (50) Highways; their record department usually carries a good selection of Hawaiian music. Outstanding Hawaiian musicians are listed in *The Essential Guide to O'ahu*; the music of Kaua'i's most famous pop singer to date, Glenn Medeiros, is available in the above stores.

GROCERIES

Those visitors with kitchen facilities may not choose to eat out for every meal. Local supermarkets carry most of the standard items that you're used to, and a lot more, including large sections of Oriental staples and standards. Some visitors find a tour of the large grocery stores an amazing experi-ence, especially in the produce department where you may see a number of things you don't recognize. The large supermarket chains on Kaua'i are **Big Save**, with eight locations around the island, **Star Market** in Kukui Grove Center and **Foodland** at Princeville, Waipouli and Lihue Shopping

Center. The Waipouli Foodland is open twenty-four hours a day, seven days a week. Delightful vestiges of a bygone era are the genuine old general stores such as **Puhi Store** and **Matsuura Store** on the South Shore and **Wainiha General Store** on the North Shore. Favorite local snack foods found in most stores (and packable to take or send home) are: Waimea taro chips, Kauai Kookies, Hawaiian Sun fruit juices, and an array of Yick Lung 'crack seed' (Oriental dried and salted fruit), as well as the famous and delectable macadamia nut, transplanted to Hawai'i from its native Australia and sold in countless presentations almost everywhere.

CONVENIENCE STORES

Menehune Food Marts are located at Kīlauea and Kalāheo; **7-Elevens** are found on Kūhiō Highway at Kapa'a, Hanamā'ulu and Līhu'e. At the Kauai Beachboy Hotel and Coco Palms Resort, the **Happy Kauaian** fills this need. The **Koloa Mill** at Old Koloa Town offers one-stop shopping, and **Brennecke's Mini Mart** at Po'ipū serves the beach goers. The **Kinipopo General Store** at Wailua is open twenty-four hours, seven days. At Kapa'a is **Pono Market**.

HEALTH FOOD STORES

The North Shore's health food emporium is **Hanalei Health & Natural Foods** in Ching Young Village.

On the East Shore, it's **Ambrose's Kapuna Natural Foods** in Waipouli, and the South Shore is served from Līhu'e by **Hale O' Health** in the Rice Shopping Center and **General Nutrition Center** in Kukui Grove Center. A popular local health-food item available in many stores around the island is Anahola Granola.

DRUGSTORES

The largest drugstores are **Longs** at Kukui Grove Center and **Pay 'n Save**, also in Līhu'e. Both of these are the type of drugstore that sells everything under the sun. **HPI Pharmacy** and **Lihue Pharmacy** in Līhu'e, **Shoreview Pharmacy** in Kapa'a and **Westside Pharmacy** in Hanapēpē offer all the standard drugstore services on a smaller scale.

DINING

The 50 best restaurants
Fast foods
Bakeries
Shave ice

FINE and FUN DINING

DINING

K
auaʻi offers a surprisingly large selection of diverse dining experiences, and even a few world-class restaurants. From haute cuisine to ice cream, the Garden Island has plenty to offer, and you can pick a venue to suit almost any mood.

THE 50th STATE'S 50 BEST RESTAURANTS ON KAUA'I

A selection of choice dining establishments is listed here, ranked in order of quality and price. A complete list, categorized by cuisine, is included as an appendix at the back of this book.

The following symbols will assist you in choosing a restaurant to suit your requirements, your taste and your budget.

Price ranges indicated are per person and do not include drinks. Most Fine Dining restaurants accept major credit cards; most Fun Dining listings do not.

B	Breakfast
L	Lunch
D	Dinner
R	Reservations suggested
E	Entertainment/dancing
W	Wheelchair access

$$$$	$40 +
$$$	$30-$40
$$	$15-$30
$	$10-$15

Fine dining

The following criteria were used in evaluating the quality of the restaurants rated below:
- taste, texture and presentation of food
- attentiveness and demeanor of service staff
- price in relation to food
- appropriateness of menu selec tions
- china and napery
- decor and lighting
- building and setting
- ambience and mood
- an indefinable essence that inspires a feeling of specialness

★★★★★
FIVE-STAR RESTAURANTS

Midori $$$$ R / D   W

Quiet nook with elegant Japanese decor, impeccable service, superbly-flavored and artfully-presented continental cuisine with some unusual Island and Asian touches: seafood, beef, lamb and poultry; light sauces enhance without overwhelming. Select list of fine wines. Delicious desserts. Kauai Hilton, Waipouli 245-1955

Nobles $$$$ R E / D   W

Exceptionally elegant dining room with an air of quiet intimacy and discreet opulence. Creative continental cuisine includes seafood, lamb, poultry, beef and game. Menu is *prix fixe*, offering appetizer, soup *or* salad, main course, extraordinary dessert and coffee or gourmet tea. Wine list offers vast selection of domestic and French wines. Service almost perfect. Closed Sunday and Monday. Sheraton Princeville, Hanalei 826-9644

The Tamarind $$$$ R / D   W

Brass columns, dark woods, pale silken cushions create ambience of luxury. Diverse culinary creations include seafood, poultry, beef and lamb; sauces are well-seasoned but tend to be thick and too generously applied unless served separately. Friendly waiters and *sommelier* are attentive and helpful. Extensive and diverse wine list; small selection of excellent desserts or feather-light souffle of the day. Waiohai Resort, Po'ipū 742-9511

★★★★
FOUR-STAR RESTAURANTS

Hale Kapa $$$ R / D   W

French country kitchen decor, with harvest displays of breads, pastas and herbs, cast-iron chandeliers, brick arches, framed Hawaiian quilts. Elegant service and presentation; uncooked portions of steak, seafood and poultry are presented for personal inspection by waiter explaining preparation of each. Grilled meats served on rather than under delicately flavored sauces, artfully presented lightly-cooked vegetables. Excellent wine list; Nobles wine list also available. Sheraton Princeville, Hanalei 826-9644

Waiohai Terrace $-$$$ R / B L D   W

Open, oceanfront terrace offering sweeping views of Po'ipū Beach. Basket of specialty breads at breakfast includes best banana bread ever. Sandwiches and light meals at lunch; fresh fruit plate with ginger sauce for dipping is exceptional. Dinner includes well-prepared fresh seafood, steak and poultry. Excellent wine list with access to Tamarind cellars, next door. Sunday brunch (10am-2pm) features every sort of seafood, meat, salad, pastry and pie; omelettes and crepes of all types made to order. Waiohai Resort, Po'ipū 742-9511

THREE-STAR RESTAURANTS

Charo's Restaurant $$ R / L D   W
Attentive and friendly service in casual Hawaiian oceanfront setting. Lunch offers interesting choice of sandwiches and salads; dinner excels in fresh seafood and beef. Giant shrimp breaded in macadamia nut meal with sesame/ginger sauce is special. Good wine list and desserts. Adjacent to Hanalei Colony Resort, 5-7132 Kūhiō Hwy, Hā'ena 826-6422

Shell House $/$$ B L D   W
Popular bar/eating house right on the main road offers no atmosphere, but excellent food. Diverse menu, ample portions keep it crowded at breakfast, lunch and dinner; exceptional clam chowder and dinner seafood specialties. Sunday brunch. Kūhiō Hwy (56) at Aku Road, Hanalei 826-7977

TWO-STAR RESTAURANTS

Bali Hai $/$$ R E / B L D   W
Usual steak and seafood fare; view overlooking Hanalei Bay from all tables; high ceiling hung with lovely, long batik panels. Service polite and attentive. Hanalei Bay Resort, Princeville 826-6522

Beach House $$/$$$ R / D
Oceanside bar/eatery with fabulous view is pretty, pink and green slice of southern California. Menu items mostly steak and seafood with several specials of the house. Fish is fresh and tasty, prime rib slices too thin but well-cooked. Good salad, excellent house dressing; clever ice cream creations. Service hasty and harried. Spouting Horn Road, Po'ipū 742-7575

Beamreach $$ R / D
Nautically appointed dining room known for its excellent steak and seafood. Huge salad in a wooden bowl is served with fresh, warm bread and a bowl of croutons. Wines and desserts are adequate. Service is patchy. Pali Ke Kua, Princeville 826-9131

Cafe Hanalei $-$$$ R E / B L D   W
Perched on a cliff above Hanalei Bay, with the most beautiful views in the world. Bright green and white decor evokes informal plantation mood. Flavorful food, with breakfast buffet, salads and sandwiches at lunchtime and seafood, steak and poultry for dinner. Friendly but patchy pervice. Sheraton Princeville, Hanalei 826-9644

Lagoon Dining Room $-$$$ E / B L D   W

Open-air dining room beside tranquil lagoon, looking out across huge grove of coconut palms. Sumptuous breakfast buffet and diverse morning menu selection. Interesting lunch and dinner items such as chicken baked in a green coconut, in addition to steak and seafood favorites. Early evening diners can watch torchlighting ceremony. Coco Palms Resort Hotel, Wailua 822-4921

The Outrigger Room $/$$ R E / B L D   W

Spectacular views of Po'ipū Beach from every table. Buffet or menu choices for breakfast; lunch or dinner offers international cuisine and an array of scrumptious desserts. Seafood buffet two nights per week. Good service, even under pressure of crowds. Sheraton-Kauai Hotel, Po'ipū 742-1661

ONE-STAR RESTAURANTS

107

DINING

Casa Italiana $$ R / L D

Open-air pasta emporium offers no less than fifteen varieties of the semolina art in half a dozen standard sauces, all tasty and well-prepared. Chef specializes in veal dishes and minestrone. Salad bar and wine and dessert choices are limited. Service attentive but rushed. 2989 Halekō Road, Līhu'e 245-9586

Dolphin $$/$$$ D   W

Rustic setting near riverbank with fresh breezes. Preparation of varied menu items at this longtime local seafood favorite varies with rotating roster of chefs. Good salad in enormous wooden bowl accompanied by garlic croutons and warm bread from Jacques Bakery. Service friendly but frenzied when full. Well-selected wine list. Kūhiō Hwy (56) near Hanalei River Bridge, Hanalei 826-6113

Gaylord's $$/$$$ R / L D

Tables set around open veranda of old plantation estate provide an elegant setting. Menu reads like a dream, but any other than the plainest dishes are apt to be disappointing; seasoning very uneven. Good salads and sandwiches. Excellent chocolate/amaretto mousse. Servers rush around. Good wine list. Kilohana Plantation, Kaumuali'i Hwy, Puhi 245-9593

Green Garden   B L D   W

Family-run restaurant a local legend; constantly crowded due to its wide selection of excellent, inexpensive food including Hawaiian, Portuguese, Japanese, Chinese and American fare. Famous pies, fast service. 13749 Kaumuali'i Hwy, Hanapēpē 335-5422

NO-STAR RESTAURANTS

Casa di Amici $$/$$$ L D   W

Beautiful open-air room with clay fountain, dark green tables, wicker chairs. Several types of pasta are offered in large or small portions with a variety of sauces; veal, fish and chicken. Bland tomato sauce, pasta soggy if not ordered *al dente*. Good salad and selection of Italian wines. Superlative cheesecakes and espresso coffee. Kong Lung Center, 2484 Keneke Street, Kīlauea 828-1388

Eggbert's   B L D

No-nonsense eatery providing solid food, modest prices and no atmosphere. Omelette specialists; lunch and dinner are standard fare. Service prompt and friendly. 4483 Rice Street, Līhu'e 245-6325

Ho's Garden $$$ L D   W

Tiny Chinese restaurant in the heart of town; no atmosphere, excellent food at low prices. Large selection of Cantonese cuisine. 3016 'Umi Street, Līhu'e 245-5255

I'ulani Isle $ B L D

Unpretentious dining room with lush tropical setting. Pleasant for breakfast; lunch and dinner specialties Italian and seafood. Friendly service, modest prices. After 9pm live music in adjacent bar. Princeville Shopping Center, Hanalei 826-7680

Kokee Lodge   B L D

Pleasant dining room with standard fare, only restaurant for many miles, near the end of the road to the lookout points over Kalalau Valley. Good food and service. Kōke'e State Park, Kekaha 335-6061

Kountry Kitchen   B L D   W

Great spot for big breakfast eaters, known for its tasty, crepe-like, rolled omelettes with many filling choices. Lunch includes salads, sandwiches and meals; dinner offers good variety of seafood, beef and poultry choices. 1485 Kūhiō Hwy, Kapa'a 822-3511

UNRATED RESTAURANTS

Atami $ D

Tiny, air-conditioned restaurant, tucked away in a shopping center, has reputation for excellent Japanese cuisine. No credit cards. 4-901 Kūhiō Hwy, Wailua 822-1642

Club Jetty $ R E / D   W

Popular family restaurant overlooking Nāwiliwili Harbor is Kaua'i institution; serves luscious Cantonese cuisine along with a few American dinners. After 9pm becomes a hard-rocking nightclub. Closed Sundays. Nāwiliwili Harbor, Līhu'e 245-4970

Hanamaulu Cafe and Tea Room $-$$$ R / L D

Well-known for a wide variety of superb Japanese and Chinese food, served at low tables in gracious tea rooms around a carp pond or in the restaurant with table-top grills and a sushi bar. Closed Mondays. Kūhiō Hwy, Hanamā'ulu 245-2511

Inn on the Cliffs $$/$$$ L D   W

Multi-level, glass enclosed, wood paneled restaurant perched on cliffside overlooking Nāwiliwili Bay. Entry at top provides lounge/patio with piano music. Pasta and fresh seafood specialties. Westin Kauai, Līhu'e 245-5050

Jacaranda Terrace $-$$$ E / B L D   W

Lovely, airy dining room off the hotel lobby provides a casual setting with beautiful garden/ocean view. Serving international and Island favorites. Good wine list. Kauai Hilton, Waipouli 245-1955

Keoki's Paradise $/$$ R / D

Torchlit tables, arranged around a landscaped lagoon. Fresh fish specialties and a variety of beef cuts and seafood/beef combinations, plus Kōloa-style pork ribs. Seafood and Taco Bar with lots of *pūpūs.* Good wine list. Kiahuna Shopping Village, Po'ipū 742-7534

Kiibo $/$$ L D

Tasteful Japanese fare, good variety of choices, tempura specialty: ingredients can be ordered a la carte. No credit cards. 2991 'Umi Street, Līhu'e 245-2650

Kintaro $$ R / D

Elegant Japanese setting and cuisine with a wide range of sushi, sashimi and tempura plus several beef choices. 4-370 Kūhiō Hwy, Wailua 822-3341

The Masters $$$/$$$$ R J / D   W

Mauve tones, French lace, harp music and romantic views of torchlit fountains provide elegant atmosphere for savoring the creations of masterful French chefs, with an occasional touch of the Far East. Menu offers two *prix fixe* options as well as *a la carte.* Exceptional wine list. Closed Sunday. Kauai Lagoons Golf and Racquet Club, Westin Kauai, Līhu'e 245-5050

Plantation Gardens $$ R / D   W

Verandas of gracious old home in lovely garden provide one of the most romantic dining settings on the island. Seafood specialists offering several kinds of fresh fish daily and a few beef choices. Good wine list. Kiahuna Plantation Resort, Po'ipū 742-1695

DINING

110

Tempura Garden $$$ L D   W / D

Chefs from Kyoto present the finest in Japanese culinary tradition—*Kyoto Kaiseki*. Handed down from the Heian period when Japanese court life was at its apex, this presentation of several courses is high art. Tempura, sushi and sashimi are also available. Set in Japanese gardens with waterfalls and *koi* ponds. Westin Kauai, Lihu'e 245-5050

Voyage Room $$-$$$$ B L D   W

Spacious restaurant overlooking the hotel garden; quality of food varies; buffet or extensive menu, diverse salad bar. Expensive wine list. Sheraton Coconut Beach, Kapa'a 822-3455

Fun dining

In addition to world-class fine dining, Kaua'i offers myriad eating experiences that provide taste treats and just plain fun, especially for families. Lu'aus are listed under ENTERTAINMENT.

Barbecue Inn   R / B L D

Highly recommended by local residents, this unpretentious eatery serves far more than barbecue, offering a wide variety of beef, seafood and poultry choices in generous portions at modest prices. No credit cards. 2982 Kress Street, Lihu'e 245-2921

Brennecke's Beach Broiler   R / L D

Upstairs, casual dining room overlooking Po'ipu Beach. Seafood, beef, poultry and pasta; fresh fish is the best. Small, well-selected wine list. Surfing movies with a huge variety of *pupus* at 10pm. 2100 Ho'one Road, Po'ipu 742-7588

The Bull Shed $ D

Prime rib, steaks, rack of lamb, seafood. Kapa'a location in spectacular waterfront setting. No reservations accepted. 796 Kuhio Hwy, Kapa'a 822-3791; Harbor Village Shopping Center, Lihu'e 245-4551

Carriage House $/$$ E / D

Pay-as-you enter plantation cookout offering grilled steak, ribs, fish and chicken along with an unusually varied salad bar and plenty of baked beans. Large, open-air dining room; live music. Kilohana Plantation, Puhi 245-9593

Hamura Saimin   L

Super-cheap prices for superb soup and saimin, cash only, take-out orders. 2956 Kress Street, Lihu'e 245-3271

JJ's Broiler $/$$ R / D

Beef specialties, also chicken and fish. Quality uneven. 2971 Haleko Road, Lihu'e 245-3841. Same menu at JJ's **Boiler Room**, Coconut Plantation Marketplace, Kapa'a 822-4411

Kauai Chop Suey   L D

Clean, bright dining room in red and white with Chinese lanterns. Delicious Chinese specialties; slow service, low prices. Take-out orders. No credit cards. Closed Mondays. Harbor Village Shopping Center, Līhu'e 245-8790

Koloa Fish & Chowder House $/$$ R / L D

Extensive variety of excellent seafood, both local and imported, and prime rib. Quality of bread and vegetables not as good. Expensive wine list. No credit cards. Old Koloa Town 742-7377

Norberto's El Cafe   D

Highly-praised Mexican eatery, especially noted for burritos, tostadas and chilis rellenos. Cantina decor, friendly service. 4-1373 Kūhiō Hwy, Kapa'a 822-3362

Ono Family Restaurant   B L D

Generous servings of inexpensive, plain food, with a few interesting, well-prepared house specials. Slow but friendly service. Cozy atmosphere. Closed Sunday evenings. 4-1292 Kūhiō Hwy, Kapa'a 822-1710

Prince Bill's $$/$$$ B D   W

Spectacular ocean views from top of Kaua'i's tallest building afford fun setting for fine food. Lavish breakfast/brunch buffet; also *a la carte*. Dinner *prix fixe* menu only; grilled steak and seafood. Westin Kauai, Līhu'e 245-5050

Rosita's $ R / L D

Rated tops for Mexican food by local residents, the menu also includes hamburgers, steaks, fish, chicken, pork, lasagna. Service variable. Kukui Grove Shopping Center, Līhu'e 245-8561

Sharon's Saimin   L D

Tiny restaurant serving giant bowls of steaming and scrumptious saimin at remarkably low prices; take-out orders are smaller to fit in the containers. No credit cards. 4-129 Kūhiō Hwy, Kapa'a 822-5140

Tahiti Nui Cocktail Lounge and Restaurant $ R / D

A bit of old Kaua'i in the heart of Hanalei town, this tiny restaurant with adjacent bar offers a small selection of exceptionally delectable fare; on Monday, Wednesday and Friday evenings they stage a lu'au. Kūhiō Hwy, Hanalei 826-6277

Tropical Taco   L D

Pink stucco cantina, an extension of the famous green van parked at Hanalei; eat-in or take-out Mexican food; bland seasonings; cabbage instead of lettuce changes taste of typical Mexican fare. Kapaa Shopping Center, Kūhiō Hwy, Kapa'a 822-3622

DINING

111

DINING

FAST FOODS

New on the Kauaʻi fast-food scene is a hot dog emporium with miniature golf course called **Mustard's Last Stand**, offering a dozen delicious varieties of this sausage treat with a salad-bar size condiment counter where you pile on your choice of the many mustards, relishes, cheeses, sauerkraut and chili in whatever quantity you like. They also serve breakfast 'doggie muffins' (scrambled eggs, sausage and cheese on a locally-baked sesame seed bun) or doughnuts, and Lappert's ice cream. **Waipouli Delicatessen and Restaurant** is a quick service luncheonette-style eatery serving eat-in or take-out orders of American and Oriental favorites. A local-brand pizzeria, **Brick Oven Pizza** makes excellent pizzas and hero-type Italian sandwiches.

Zippy's, a home-grown chain of local-style, quick-service eateries specializing in Hawaiian 'plate lunch' combinations and found all over Honolulu, has but a single location in Līhuʻe. The same is true for Mainland fast-food giant, **Wendy's**. **McDonald's** and **Pizza Hut** have two locations each and **Dairy Queen** has three locations. For addresses and phone numbers, see the Restaurant Appendix at the back of this book.

COOKBOOKS

Those doing their own cooking might wish to try some local recipes, taking advantage of the ready availabilty of all the ingredients—which are hard to come by in some areas and climates. Many such cookbooks are sold at local bookstores and souvenir shops. Island Heritage has published three collections of local recipes which we can recommend: *Favorite Recipes from Hawaii, Tropical Drinks and Pupus from Hawaii* and *Entertaining Island Style.*

BAKERIES

Without doubt, the most famous bakery on Kauaʻi is **Jacques** in Kīlauea. Numerous Kauaʻi restaurants serve this bread and several fine Honolulu restaurants fly his fresh breads to Oʻahu daily. The reputation is well deserved. The variety is impressive and the quality superb. Some of Kauaʻi's hotels have fine bakeries of their own—notably the Waiohai and the Sheraton Princeville—and these will sometimes take special orders for whole loaves of your favorite variety.

The spreading fame of the **Kauai Kookie Kompany**, of Hanapēpē (their products can be bought in most grocery stores on Kauaʻi and in many on other Hawaiian islands), has sparked competition by other island bakers. **Popo's** Cookies at Waipouli produces something very similar, but **Crumb's Bakery** has gone far beyond. Even **Lappert's**, of Hanapēpē ice cream fame, has gotten into the act with a line of clones that should bring a worried frown to the brow of Mrs Fields. Lappert's Old Koloa Town shop has started producing, in addition to cookies, both giant and normal-size muffins in several delectable varieties that are worth going out of your way for and they have a few tables if you wish to eat on the spot.

Kaua'i also seems to be running a competition for the world's best *liliko'i* [passion fruit] chiffon pie. Many restaurants bake their own and some will sell whole pies. Among the strongest contenders for the title are **Omoide's** and **Green Garden**, both in Hanapēpē.

Kauai Kitchens specializes in *malasadas* (sugared doughnuts without a hole) and Portuguese sweet bread and has several locations with tables on the premises. **Sweet Temptations** (826-9004) in the Princeville Shopping Center specializes in breads, pastries and desserts and also makes sandwiches at lunchtime.

The **Tip Top Bakery** in Līhu'e bakes a delightful variety of breads and pastries, and **The Village Snack & Bakery Shop** in Hanalei also offers a wide range of scrumptious baked goodies.

NUTS, CANDIES and JAMS

One of Hawai'i's famous edibles are macadamia nuts, brought to the islands from Australia, and the succulent kernels are available roasted and salted or laced with an imaginative array of coatings—in addition to the standard chocolate, coffee and honey—in many gift and souvenir shops all over the island. A specialist in these as well as other sweet treats like tropical fruit jams, jellies and syrups is **The Nut Cracker Sweet** (822-4811) at Coconut Plantation Marketplace.

ICE CREAM and YOGURT

The number one ice cream vendor in Kaua'i is **Lappert's Ice Cream Parlor**, which began as a small shop in Hanapēpē and has become so popular and successful that it has expanded to all the Hawaiian islands, and even to California! They produce many flavors and are continually inventing more. No one should leave Kaua'i without trying this gourmet treat.

Zack's Famous Frozen Yogurt with locations in Kiahuna Shopping Village and Līhu'e offers a lower-calorie cool snack, as does the **Yogurt Patio**, in Waipouli and the Kukui Grove Center. For something different and delectable, go to **Banana Joe's Fruit Stand** on Kūhiō Highway near Kalihiwai on the North Shore for a fruit smoothie, which is frozen banana, papaya or pineapple, spun to a light ice.

SHAVE ICE

The endemic treat that can't be packed and shipped home from Kaua'i is 'shave ice'. This finely-shaved ice with flavored syrup poured over it closely resembles what is generally known on the Mainland as 'snow cones', but it *isn't* the same. The texture of shave ice is much finer—more like actual snow, and the rainbow version is a delight to behold as well as to consume. On a hot afternoon, this treat is ultra-refreshing. Some vendors will add a scoop of ice cream or sweet black beans under the mound of delicate ice shavings for a double treat. Shave ice can be purchased from many places all over the island, including refreshment vans parked near beaches.

ACCOMMODATION

The best hotels on Kaua'i
Condominiums and apartments
Homes and cottages
Cabins and campsites

ACCOMMODATION

Kaua'i's best hotels are described and rated below, followed by notations of other types of lodging. While most people think automatically of hotels and condominiums when seeking lodging for their vacations, there are, in fact, several alternatives—such as vacation homes and cottages, camping cabins and private bed and breakfast situations.

THE 50th STATE'S BEST HOTELS ON KAUA'I

The ratings below indicate the quality of selected hotels on Kaua'i. The criteria for a *good* hotel are simple: comfort, courtesy and cleanliness. In a *great* hotel, different things make different properties outstanding; our evaluations are based on the following criteria:

- architecture, decor, grounds and view
- well-trained, responsible and caring staff
- personalized consideration from manager, *concierge* and *maitre d'*, prompt room service, attention to details
- amenities and niceties such as fluffy towels, extra pillows, newspaper and wake-up coffee, flowers, beauty salons and shops
- fine dining, all-day restaurant and food service, poolside grazing
- most importantly, an indefinable, warm, pleasing ambience

Unless you're traveling during the busy winter months (January through April; February at peak), reservations shouldn't be a problem.

Room rates are seasonal, with the winter months fetching higher prices. The price ranges of the hotels listed are categorized as follows:

$$$$	luxury class
$$$	$100-$200+
$$	$70-$100
$	$35-$70
No $	budget

W   **Wheelchair access**

★★★★
FOUR-STAR HOTELS

Sheraton Princeville $$$/$$$$ W

Spectacular cliffside setting overlooking Hanalei Bay, 300 rooms, all but 15 which have ocean views (those 15 overlook the 36-hole Princeville golf course); air conditioning, tennis courts, swimming pool, beach, meeting rooms, shops, cocktail lounges, disco, 3 restaurants: 5-, 4- and 2★. Building constructed in several levels that fit nicely into the hillside without spoiling the natural beauty of the area. End of Kahauku Road, Princeville. PO Box 3069, Princeville 826-9644 (800 227-4700)

The Westin Kauai at Kauai Lagoons $$$/$$$$ W

Kaua'i's newest resort hotel. Beachfront setting, overlooking Nāwiliwili Harbor, 850 rooms, air conditioning, beach, swimming pool, two 18-hole golf courses, 8 tennis courts, fitness center, shops, 7 restaurants, 3 lounges, extensive gardens and lagoons with wildlife, horse-drawn carriages, wedding chapel, meeting rooms. Kalapaki Beach, Līhu'e 245-5050 (800 228-3000)

★★★
THREE-STAR HOTELS

Coco Palms Resort Hotel $$-$$$$ W

Romantic setting in coconut grove, 416 rooms, cottages and suites, all air-conditioned, some with lava tubs, giant clamshell washbasins and canoe beds. Two stories of shops, 3 pools, 9 tennis courts, 2 paddle tennis courts, museum, zoo, library, wedding chapel. Dining rooms beside lagoon, nightly torchlighting ceremony. Across from Wailua Beach. PO Box 631, Līhu'e 822-4921 (800 542-2626)

Kauai Hilton $$$ W

Kawailoa beachfront setting, 350 rooms, air conditioning, swimming pool, adjacent golf course and tennis courts, shop, 3 restaurants (including a 5★), disco; adjacent condominium resort. 4331 Kaua'i Beach Drive, Waipouli 245-1955 (800 445-8667)

Sheraton-Kauai $$$/$$$$ W

Beachfront, 340 rooms and suites, each with private *lānai*, air conditioning, all-suite ocean wing ★★★★, 2 lagoons, 2 swimming pools with poolside bar and snacks; beach, 4 restaurants, lounge, shops, meeting rooms; nearby golf, tennis and shopping village. Po'ipū Beach 742-1661 (800 325-3535)

Stouffer Waiohai Beach Resort $$$/$$$$ W

Beachfront, 413 rooms, a number of which are dark due to W shape of building, and 21 luxurious suites; air conditioning, 2 swimming pools (1 with semi-sunken bar) and a wading pool, beach, fitness center, 6 tennis courts, adjacent golf course, 2 restaurants (including a 5- and 4★), lounge, shops. Po'ipū Beach, RR1, PO Box 174, Kōloa 742-9511 (800 227-4700)

ACCOMMODATION

TWO-STAR HOTELS

Sheraton Coconut Beach $$$/$$$$ W

Waipouli beachfront, 309 rooms, air conditioning, beach, swimming pool, tennis courts, restaurant, lounge, shops; adjacent shopping village, nearby golf course. Coconut Plantation, Kapa'a 822-3455 (800 325-3535)

Poipu Beach Hotel $$-$$$$ W

Beachfront, 139 rooms, air conditioning, beach, swimming pool, tennis courts, shops, restaurants and lounges; use of adjacent Waiohai's fitness center, nearby golf course and shopping village. Po'ipū Beach, RR1, PO Box 174, Kōloa 742-1681 (800 227-4700)

ONE-STAR HOTELS

118

Kauai Resort $-$$$ W

Oceanfront at mouth of Wailua River, 242 rooms, air conditioning, beach at adjacent Lydgate Park, restaurant, lounge, shops, meeting rooms, nearby golf course.   3-5920 Kūhiō Hwy, Kapa'a 245-3931 (800 367-5004)

Islander on the Beach $/$$

Beachfront, 199 rooms and 1 studio apartment, air conditioning, swimming pool, beach, shops.   484 Kūhiō Hwy, Kapa'a 822-7417 (800 367-5124)

Kauai Beachboy $/$$

Waipouli beachfront, 243 rooms, air conditioning, swimming pool, wading pool, beach, volleyball, tennis, restaurant, lounge, disco, adjacent shopping village, nearby golf course. Coconut Plantation, Kapa'a 822-3441 (800 227-4700)

Kauai Sands $/$$

Waipouli beachfront, 200 rooms, air conditioning, beach, swimming pool, restaurant, lounge, meeting rooms, shops; adjacent shopping village, nearby golf course. 420 Papaloa Road, Kapa'a 822-4951 (800 367-7000)

UNRATED HOTELS

Hotel Coral Reef   W

Kapa'a beachfront, 26 rooms, no room telephones, beach, swimming pool at adjacent Kapa'a Beach Park, near shops and restaurants. 1516 Kūhiō Hwy, Kapa'a 822-4481 (800 843-4659)

Kauai Inn   w

Wooded setting on edge of Hule'ia National Wildlife Refuge, 48 rooms, some with water views across Niumalu Beach Park; between Nāwiliwili Harbor and Alakoko (Menehune) Fishpond. Niumalu Road, Līhu'e 245-3316 (800 367-8047 x243)

Oceanview Motel

Opposite Nāwiliwili Park, 21 rooms with refrigerators, no room telephones, beach nearby. 3445 Wilcox Road, Līhu'e 245-6345

Hale Lihue Motel

Central Līhu'e, 20 rooms, partial air conditioning, parking. 2931 Kalena Street, Līhu'e 245-3151/2751

Hale Pumehana

Central Līhu'e, 17 motel rooms, no room telephones, partial air conditioning, shop, parking. 3083 'Akāhi Street, Līhu'e (PO Box 1828) 245-2106/6151

Tip Top Motel

Central Līhu'e, 34 motel rooms, air conditioning, restaurant and bakery, lounge, meeting room, parking. 3173 'Akāhi Street, Līhu'e 245-2333/2761

CONDOMINIUMS and APARTMENTS

A more at-home atmosphere is available in self-contained apartments, and these are very popular, particularly for vacationers and business travelers staying several weeks. Apartment sizes vary, as do amenities and furnishings. Price ranges shown are the same as those for hotels. The places listed here, unrated and in alphabetical order, are members of the Hawai'i Visitors Bureau; there are many more units of this type available through real estate and property management agents on Kaua'i. Many vacation rental apartments are individually owned, and several companies may represent the various owners in any given complex.

Alii Kai I $$$

Princeville complex, 59 two-bedroom apartments, most with ocean views; swimming pool, golf, tennis. 826-9921 (800 367-8047 x251)

Alii Kai II $$

In Princeville on Hanalei Bluff, 56 two-bedroom apartments, some with ocean views, restaurant, lounge, swimming pool, tennis, golf. 826-9988

Cliffs $$$

Oceanfront Princeville complex, 205 one- and two-bedroom apartments, most with ocean views, swimming pool, meeting room, golf, tennis. 826-9833 (800 367-8047 x251)

The resort community of Princeville lies adjacent to Hanalei Bay.

CONDOMINIUMS and APARTMENTS

Hale Moi $$

Princeville complex overlooking golf course, 40 apartments, some with ocean view, golf, tennis. 826-9833 (800 367-8047 x251)

Hanalei Bay Resort $-$$$

Princeville complex, 280 studio, one-, two- and three-bedroom apartments, many with ocean views, golf, tennis, swimming pool, 2★ restaurant, lounge, shops, meeting room. 826-9833/6522 (800 367-8047 x251; 800 854-8843; California 800 472-8449; Canada 800 824-8968)

Hanalei Colony Resort $$/$$$

Hā'ena beachfront complex, 52 two-bedroom apartments, some overlooking the ocean, no room telephones, swimming pool, 3★ Charo's Restaurant next door. 826-6235 (800 367-8047 x148)

Ka'eo Kai $$$

Princeville complex, 64 two- and three-bedroom apartments, no ocean views, swimming pool, golf, tennis. 826-7204/9833 (800 367-8047 x251)

Kaha Lani $$/$$$

East Shore beachfront complex, 74 one-, two- and three-bedroom apartments, ceiling fans, swimming pool, beach, tennis. 822-9331 (800 367-5124)

Kapaa Sands $/$$

Wailua oceanfront complex, 24 studio and two-bedroom apartments, swimming pool, tennis, golf, shops, restaurant, lounge. 822-4901 (800 222-4901)

Kapaa Shore $/$$

Oceanfront complex, 81 one- and two-bedroom apartments, partial air conditioning, no room telephones, swimming pool, tennis. 822-3055 (800 367-7040; 800 854-8843; California 800 472-8449; Canada 800 824-8968)

Kauai Hilton Beach Villas $$$

Kawailoa beachfront setting, 150 one- and two-bedroom apartments with complete kitchen and laundry facilities plus maid service; all facilities and amenities of adjacent Kauai Hilton Hotel including swimming pool, golf course and tennis courts, shop, 3 restaurants (one a 5★), disco. 245-1955 (800 445-8667)

Kiahuna Plantation $$-$$$$

Po'ipū beachfront complex set in expansive gardens, 333 one- and two-bedroom apartments, swimming pool, golf, tennis, meeting room, shop, restaurant, lounge. 742-6411/7262 (800 367-7052/7040)

Lae Nani $$/$$$

Wailua beachfront complex, 87 one- and two-bedroom apartments, ceiling fans, swimming pools, tennis. 822-4938 (800 367-6046; 800 854-8843; California 800 472-8449; Canada 800 824-8968)

CONDOMINIUMS and APARTMENTS

Makahuena at Poipu $$-$$$$

South Shore complex, 78 one-, two- and three-bedroom apartments, partial ceiling fans, swimming pool, tennis. 742-7474 (800 367-8047 x251)

Mauna Kai $$/$$$

Princeville complex, 26 two-bedroom apartments, no ocean views, swimming pool, golf. 826-9833 (800 367-8047 x251)

Nihi Kai Villas $$

South Shore complex, 70 two-bedroom apartments, swimming pool, tennis. 742-6458 (800 331-8076)

Pali Ke Kua $$

Princeville complex, cliffside setting, 98 one- and two-bedroom apartments, almost all with ocean views; swimming pool, golf, 2☆ restaurant, lounge; near Sheraton Princeville Hotel. 826-9066/9833 (800 367-7042/8047 x251)

Paniolo $$

Princeville complex, 26 one-bedroom apartments, no ocean views. 826-9833 (800 367-8047 x251)

Plantation Hale $$

Coconut Plantation complex, 160 one-bedroom apartments, swimming pool, beach, restaurants and shops at adjacent Coconut Plantation Marketplace. 822-4941 (800 367-6046)

Poipu Kai $$$/$$$$

Po'ipū beachfront complex, 275 one-, two- and three-bedroom apartments, swimming pools, beach, tennis, meeting room, restaurant, lounge. 742-6464 (800 367-6046)

Poipu Kapili $$$

At Po'ipū Beach, 60 one- and two-bedroom apartments, swimming pool, tennis. 742-6449 (800 367-8047 x105)

Poipu Shores $$

South Shore setting, 30 one-, two- and three-bedroom apartments, swimming pool, tennis. 742-6522 (800 367-5686/5687)

Pono Kai $$/$$$

East Shore beachfront setting, 217 one- and two-bedroom apartments, swimming pool, beach, tennis. 822-9831 (800 367-5124)

Prince Kuhio Rentals $

South Shore setting, 69 studio and one-bedroom apartments, swimming pool. 742-1409

CONDOMINIUMS and APARTMENTS

Puamana $$/$$$

Princeville complex, 98 two- and three-bedroom apartments, swimming pool, meeting room, golf. 826-9833 (800 367-8047 x251)

Pu'u Po'a $$$

Seaside bluff setting, 56 condominium apartments, all with ocean views, swimming pool, golf, tennis, next to Sheraton Princeville Hotel. 826-9833/9066 (800 367-7042/8047 x251)

Sandpiper Village $

Princeville complex, 74 two- and three-bedroom apartments, swimming pool, golf. 826-9613 (800 525-1166)

Sealodge $$/$$$

Princeville oceanfront complex, 86 one- and two-bedroom apartments, almost all with ocean views, swimming pool, golf course. 826-9833 (800 367-8047 x251; 800 854-8843; California 800 472-8449; Canada 800 622-0838)

Sunset Kahili $

Po'ipū oceanfront, 36 one- and two-bedroom apartments, swimming pool. 742-1691 (800 367-8047)

Wailua Bayview $$

East Shore oceanfront, 45 one-bedroom apartments, swimming pool, beach, restaurant, lounge. 822-3651 (800 367-2912)

HOMES and COTTAGES

There are literally hundreds of private homes and cottages on Kaua'i available as vacation rentals, some for periods as short as three or four days. Here we list, in alphabetical order, the ones that are members of the Hawai'i Visitors Bureau, though there are many more available through real estate agents and property managers on Kaua'i, listed in the Yellow Pages under Real Estate Rentals.

Albert Road House $$$

Three-bedroom home, near swimming pool, restaurants, lounges, shops, golf and tennis. 826-9833 (800 367-8047 x251)

Faye Home $$$

Bayside six-bedroom home on sand beach; separate guest cottage also available. 826-9833 (800 367-8047 x251)

Hale Kai

South Shore two-bedroom beachfront home. 742-9537 (800 247-5599)

CONDOMINIUMS and APARTMENTS

Garden Isle Cottages $-$$$
Oceanfront, 10 one- and two-bedroom cottage units; swimming pool. 742-6717

Knigge Home $$$
Princeville home, two-bedroom, near swimming pool, restaurants, lounges, shops, golf and tennis. 826-9833 (800 367-8047 x251)

Makai Club Cottages $$
Princeville cottages, swimming pool, tennis, golf. 826-6561 (800 367-7090)

Paliuli Cottages $$
North Shore, 8 cottages; near Hanalei Beach, restaurants, lounges, swimming pools, tennis, golf, shop. 826-6264

Steeb Home $$$
On Princeville golf course, three-bedroom home, nearby swimming pool, restaurant, lounge, shops, tennis, golf. 826-9833 (800 367-8047 x251)

Waimea Plantation Cottages $
West Kaua'i, 16 one- to four-bedroom cottages; beachfront, swimming pool. 338-1625 (800 992-4632)

VACATION RENTAL AGENTS

Kaua'i has about three dozen property management agents dealing with vacation rental units of various types and sizes.

A selection of those with the broadest range of properties is given here: **Aloha Rental Management** PO Box 1109, Hanalei 826-9833 (800 367-8047); **Grantham Resorts** PO Box 983, Kōloa 742-1395; **Kauai Vacation Rentals** 4480 Ahukini Road, Līhu'e 245-8841 (800 367-5025); **Bob Lloyd Realty** PO Box 99, Kōloa 742-1243 (800 826-2824); **North Shore Properties & Vacation Rentals** PO Box 607, Hanalei (800 367-8047 x331); **Prosser Realty** PO Box 367, Līhu'e 245-4711 (800 367-8047 x117); **R & R Realty** RR 1, PO Box 70, Kōloa 742-7555 (800 367-8022); **Toulon Realty** PO Box 666, Kōloa 742-6767.

BED and BREAKFAST

An increasingly popular travel option, especially on Kaua'i, is bed-and-breakfast lodging in private residences. **Bed & Breakfast Hawaii** (PO Box 449, Kapa'a 96746 822-7771) and **Pacific-Hawaii Bed & Breakfast** (19 Kai Nani Place, Kailua 96734 [on O'ahu] 262-6026) can provide information and reservations.

124

CABINS and CAMPSITES

Adventurous souls with a taste for the outdoor life favor more rustic lodging. Tent camping is permitted at some parks on Kaua'i--a fun option for families--and cabins are available at a few sites.

Private camps

Kokee Lodge, located in Kōke'e State Park, has a dozen cabins—two small, one-room units and ten two-bedroom units that sleep up to six or seven people—all completely furnished with stove, refrigerator, hot showers, crockery, cutlery, pots and pans, and linens, towels, blankets and pillows; wood for the fireplaces is available. Restaurant serves breakfast, lunch and dinner. Park rules apply, so maximum length of stay is five days. Kōke'e State Park Reservations: PO Box 819, Waimea 96796 335-6061

Nearby are **Kokee Methodist Camp** which has a lodge (335-3429), **Kokee Hongwanji Camp** (335-3444, reservations 245-6262), and the YWCA's **Camp Sloggett**, which has a bunkhouse and a lodge (reservations 245-5959, lodge 335-6060).

At Kōloa, the **Kāhili Mountain Park** (742-9921) has big cabins with kitchenettes and smaller cabins with shared shower and restroom facilities, which are also used by tent campers. On the beach at Hā'ena is the YMCA's **Camp Naue** (826-6419), which has bunkhouses and tent sites, with shared shower, restroom and kitchen facilities. The YMCA also has a hostel in Po'ipū (742-1200).

Exploring sea life at Hanalei Bay.

State parks

Permits are required for camping in State Parks, and these may be obtained at the Division of State Parks' district office on Kaua'i (3060 'Eiwa Street, Rm 208 M-F 8am-4:15pm 245-4444 or write to PO Box 1671, Līhu'e 96766).

There are no fees, but applications must include the number of persons for whom the permit is requested and their names, and camping is limited to five days in any thirty-day period.

State Parks where camping is permitted are: **Kōke'e State Park** (central mountains--four areas, Waimea and Koai'e Canyons--five areas); **Polihale State Park** (west coast); **Lydgate State Park** (east coast) and **Nā Pali Coast State Park** (north coast) in the Hanakāpī'ai, Hanakoa and Kalalau Valleys.

County beach parks

Kaua'i County camping permits are issued for four days at a time and are renewable for four days; there is a minimal charge per adult, and requests must include the number of persons for whom the permit is to be issued along with their names and their ages.

Reservations may be made by mail (Kaua'i County Parks and Recreation Department 4396 Rice Street, Līhu'e 96766), but permits must be picked up in person at the address included with your verification.

A map of the parks, available at the Department, lists the following camping areas: **Lucy Wright Beach Park**, Waimea; **Salt Pond Beach Park**, Hanapēpē; **Niumalu Beach Park**, Niumalu (on the Hule'ia River just upstream from Nāwiliwili Harbor); **Hanamā'ulu Beach Park**, Hanamā'ulu; **Anahola Beach Park**, Anahola; **'Anini Beach Park**, Kalihiwai; and **Hā'ena Beach Park**, Hā'ena. All parks have restroom facilities and showers.

ET CETERA

Other services
Traveling with children
Handicapped travelers
Other islands

OTHER SERVICES

Here we cover a miscellany of other services that did not lend themselves to appropriate inclusion in other sections of the guidebook—everything from typists to luggage repair to specialists in the arrangement of tropical nuptials.

LAUNDRY and DRY CLEANING

The need for a laundromat can be urgent, especially for hikers and campers. These are found in Līhuʻe at the junction of Kūhiō and Kaumualiʻi Highways and at **Kapaa Laundry Center** (1105J Kūhiō Hwy, Kapaʻa 822-3113).

Laundry and dry cleaning service in South Shore areas is available through **Up-To-Date Cleaners** at several locations (Līhuʻe 245-6621, Kōloa 742-1628, Hanapēpē 335-5764, Waimea 338-1032); they also offer pickup and delivery service at Princeville Center and Kinipopo Shopping Village, Wailua, through **Mail Service Center** (826-7331).

Dry cleaning is available in Kapaʻa at **Yamada's Cleaning** (822-4081). Some hotels will also handle this service for guests.

LUGGAGE and SHOE REPAIR

The Shoe Repair Shop in Līhuʻe's Kukui Grove Center (245-6543) services the leatherwork needs of the whole island.

LIBRARIES

Kauaʻi's libraries offer lending rights to visitors who obtain a local library card during their stay. Branches of the **Kauaʻi Regional Library** are located in Kapaʻa (822-5041), Līhuʻe (245-3617), Kōloa (742-1635), Hanapēpē (335-5811) and Waimea (338-1738).

BUSINESS SERVICES

Increasingly, business visitors in particular have need of secretarial and other executive services while in the Islands.

In Līhuʻe, **The Sign of the Dove** (245-3210) and **Vicky's Secretarial & Copy Services** (245-7544) offer typing, word processing and photocopying services, and **Kauai Business Services** (245-3460) offers quick copying and small printing service.

Mail Service Center in the Princeville Center (826-7331) offers mailing and copying services, as does **Mailbox Of Kauai** in Kapaʻa (822-1667), which also provides typing and word processing.

Popular among visitors is the celebrated event of getting married or renewing vows. Numerous enterprises are engaged in the business of making people's romantic dreams of tropical settings and ceremonies come true. So many spots are splendidly suited to the purpose that the difficulty is in choosing. The most famous is the Fern Grotto on the Wailua River; **Smith's Motor Boat Service** can make arrangements. There are also, of course, many lovely indoor settings, but outdoor ceremonies are overwhelmingly preferred. Some hotels have special wedding consultants on their staffs; weddings at the Coco Palms Resort are so popular that they have a chapel on the grounds, as does The Westin Kauai.

There are also companies that arrange or assist with every detail of wedding ceremonies and celebrations. Kaua'i's wedding specialists are **Brides N Roses** (4100 Rice Street, Līhu'e 245-5256) and **Wedding in Paradise** (PO Box 340, Waimea 335-3502). The latter seeks locations off the beaten wedding path and offers unusual romantic touches for that most special of occasions.

ET CETERA

129

Many couples take advantage of Kaua'i's outdoor settings as a wedding site.

POST OFFICES

Last but not least is your friendly neighborhood post office. Post office hours are: **M-F 8:00am-4:30pm Sa 8:00am-12n**. Most post offices are located on the main highway. They are located at:

Anahola (822-4710) 96703
ʻEleʻele (335-5338) 96705
Hanalei (826-6471) 96714
Hanamāʻulu (245-3851) 96715
Hanapēpē (335-5433) 96716

Kalāheo (332-8583) 96741
Kapaʻa (822-5421) 96746
Kaumakani (335-3641) 96747
Keālia (822-3181) 96751
Kekaha (337-1322) 96752
Kīlauea (828-1721) 96754
Kōloa (742-6565) 96756
Lāwaʻi (332-9161) 96765
Līhuʻe (245-4994) 96766
Makaweli (338-9921) 96769
Waimea (338-9973) 96796

TRAVELING WITH CHILDREN

Kauaʻi is an ideal destination for family vacations. Our relaxed, easygoing lifestyle, boundless outdoor activities and wholesome local entertainment provide children (and parents) with a variety of diversions, many of them also educational.

Some hotels offer daily programs for children during summer and holiday seasons, such as Sheraton Princeville. These might include hula lessons, lei making and building sandcastles. The Kauai Hilton has ongoing children's programs that introduce kids to everything from hula to origami.

In this outdoor-oriented vacationland, visits to the seashore top the list of possible family outings. The

Early signs of the surfer syndrome.

appropriateness of Kaua'i's beaches for family excursions has been thoroughly researched by frequent visitor Lenore Horowitz, and her descriptions, of great value to parents, are a major part of her book, *Kauai Underground Guide*. She also relates the experiences she and her family have had with numerous restaurants on the island. For travelers with children, this book is recommended.

HANDICAPPED TRAVELERS

There are limited special facilities for handicapped travelers on Kaua'i. The Hawai'i Commission on the Handicapped has published a brochure titled 'The Kauai Travelers Guide for Physically Handicapped Persons', which contains information about access and facilities for a number of Kaua'i points of interest, beaches and parks, shopping centers, hotels and entertainment establishments that serve the tourist industry. Copies are available from the Commission on the Handicapped (Old Federal Building, 335 Merchant Street, Rm 353, Honolulu 96813 548-7606).

TRANSPORTATION

Special transportation on Kaua'i is limited, all vans with lifts being assigned to specific program services. With advance notice, private requests may be accommodated. The **Aloha Bus** (822-9532) offers public transportation service within a limited area for disabled persons who are ambulatory. Hand controls for cars can be arranged with advance notice through **Avis Rent A Car** (245-2151). Permits for parking in restricted access zones are available from the Police Station (3060 'Umi Street, Līhu'e 96766) with a doctor's certification or a parking permit from the applicant's place of residence.

SUPPORT SERVICES

Personal care attendants, personal companions, health aides, nurse aides and voluntary companions during visits to Kaua'i are available through **Kauai Center for Independent Living** (4340 Nāwiliwili Road, Līhu'e 96766 245-4034), **G.N. Wilcox Memorial Hospital** (3420 Kūhiō Hwy, Līhu'e 96766 245-1100 x2248). For travelers older than sixty-two, the **Office of Elderly Affairs** (4396 Rice Street, Līhu'e 96766 245-4737) can provide assistance.

MEDICAL EQUIPMENT

Supplies such as wheelchairs, walkers, canes and crutches are available for sale or rental from **Bicycles Kauai** (1379 Kūhiō Hwy, Kapa'a 822-3315), **Toolmaster** (3061 Aukele Street, Līhu'e 245-8885) and

Pay 'n Save (4100 Rice Street, Līhu'e 245-6776).
A more complete range of

medical equipment can be obtained through Gims (PO Box 3118, Līhu'e 245-8966).

PHYSICIANS

The Kauai Medical Group at Wilcox Hospital (245-1500) provides

twenty-four-hour physician referral service.

OTHER ISLANDS

Each of the main Hawaiian islands has its own special magic, and *The Essential Guide to O'ahu, The Essential Guide to Maui* and *The Essential Guide to Hawai'i, the Big Island* provide the same in-depth coverage of those islands as this *Essential Guide to Kaua'i.* We hope you can visit all our islands and discover for yourself the unique charm—past and present—of each.

Just over seventeen miles west of Kaua'i, across the Kaulakahi Channel, is the small, privately owned island of Ni'ihau. Except for short helicopter tours, access to this island has been restricted to residents for well over a century. Lying sixty-three miles south of Kaua'i, across the Ka'ie'ie Channel, is the heavily populated and visited island of O'ahu, the capital of the state of Hawai'i. The island of Moloka'i, slow and uncrowded, lies nearly twenty-six miles across the Kaiwi Channel from O'ahu. Only nine miles from Moloka'i, across the Kalohi Channel, is Lāna'i, mostly owned by the Dole company and mostly planted with pineapples. The not-quite-nine-mile Pailolo Channel separates Moloka'i from Maui. Its motto, 'Maui nō ka 'oi', means 'Maui

is the best'. Tiny Kaho'olawe, not quite seven miles off the southern coast of Maui, and nearly eighteen miles southeast of Lāna'i, is inaccessible. Since 1941 it has been used by the military as a target for bombing practice, and any landing on the island by unauthorized people is prohibited. Nearly thirty miles southeast of Maui, across the 'Ale-nuihāhā Channel, is the island of Hawai'i, 'the Big Island'. Youngest in the chain, Kīlauea Volcano is still building its coastline.

Hawaiians as well as visitors travel amongst our islands often, and the high volume of traffic makes interisland air transportation eco-nomical and efficient. Flights are short, the longest taking only around half an hour. Many interisland flights connect in Honolulu, but some fly directly between islands other than O'ahu. Aloha Airlines and Hawaiian Airlines offer interisland service from Honolulu to Kaua'i's Līhu'e Airport, and Princeville Airways services Princeville Airport on the North Shore. Aloha and Hawaiian run one daily flight each directly from Kaua'i to Maui; all other interisland flights are routed through Honolulu.

APPENDIX

RENTAL AGENCIES

CAR and TRANSPORTATION

Alamo Rent A Car
Līhu'e Airport 245-8953/6576,
800 327-9633

Avis Rent A Car
Līhu'e Airport 245-3512; Princeville Airport 826-9773, 800 331-1212

Budget Rent-A-Car
Līhu'e Airport 245-4021/4572
800 527-0700

Dollar Rent A Car
Līhu'e Airport 245-4708/3651,
800 342-7398

Hertz Rent A Car
Līhu'e Airport 245-3356; Princeville Airport 826-7455, 800 654-3131

National Car Rental
Līhu'e Airport 245-3502/5636,
800 342-8431

Pedal & Paddle
Ching Young Village, Hanalei
826-9069

Rent-A-Jeep
3137A Kūhiō Hwy, Līhu'e
245-9622

Rent-A-Wreck
3156 Ho'olako St, Līhu'e 245-4755;
Līhu'e Airport 245-6411

Thrifty Rent-A-Car
4480 Ahukini Rd, Līhu'e 245-7388;
Princeville Ctr 826-6230

Tropical Rent-A-Car
3156 'Oihana St, Līhu'e 245-6988,
800 352-3923

United Car Rental
Līhu'e Airport 245-8894

134

OTHER RENTALS

Action Windsurfing
Old Koloa Town 742-6118

Aquarius Beach Center
Coconut Plantation Marketplace,
Kapa'a 822-7172

Aquatics Kauai
733 Kūhiō Hwy, Kapa'a 822-9213

Beach Activities of Kauai
Sheraton Princeville, Hanalei
826-6851

Brennecke Ocean Sports
Po'ipū Beach 742-6570

Dive Kauai
4-976 Kūhiō Hwy, Ste 4, Kapa'a
822-0452

Fathom Five Professional Divers
3450 Po'ipū Dr., Kōloa 742-6991

Hanalei Sailboards
5-5016 Kūhiō Hwy, Hanalei
826-9732

Kalapaki Beach Center
Nāwiliwili in Līhu'e 245-5955

Kauai Divers
Old Koloa Town 742-1580

Kauai Jet Ski Rentals
Kapa'a 822-7240

Kiahuna Beach Hut
Kiahuna Plantation, Po'ipū
742-6411

Ocean Odyssey Dive Shop
Kauai Hilton, Waipouli 822-9680

Pedal & Paddle
Ching Young Village, Hanalei
826-9069

Princeville Video & Beach Rentals
Princeville Ctr 826-9175

Progressive Expressions
5428 Kōloa Rd, Kōloa 742-6041

Sand People
Hanalei Trader Bldg 826-6981

Sea Sage Diving Center
  4-1378 Kūhiō Hwy, Kapaʻa 822-3841
Sea Sports Kauai
  Sheraton-Kauai, Poʻipū 742-1221
South Shore Activities
  2230 Kapili Rd, Poʻipū 742-6873
Wailua Surf & Beachwear
  4-356 Kūhiō Hwy, Wailua 822-3035

Waiohai Beach Service
  Waiohai Hotel, Poʻipū
  742-7051
Watersports Kauai
  Hanalei 826-6981
Yoshimura Store
  4597 Olohena Rd, Kapaʻa
  822-4457

PLACES OF INTEREST

Coconut Grove
  Coco Palms Resort, Wailua
  822-4921
Fern Grotto
  (Smith's Motor Boat Service Co.,
  Kapaʻa 822-4111)

Hanalei Museum
  Kūhiō Hwy, Hanalei
  826-6783
Kamokila Hawaiian Village
  6060 Kuamoʻo Rd, Kapaʻa
  822-1192

Giant mahogonies make up the Tunnel of Trees.

Kauaʻi Museum
4428 Rice St, Līhuʻe
245-6931

Kīlauea Lighthouse
end of Lighthouse Rd, Kīlauea

Kilohana
3-2087 Kaumualiʻi Hwy, Līhuʻe
245-5608

Kōkeʻe Natural History Musem
16 mile marker, Kōkeʻe Rd, Kōkeʻe
335-9975

Kukui o Lono
makai of Kaumualiʻi Hwy on Pāpālima Rd

Lutheran Church, oldest in Hawaiʻi
4602 Hoʻomana Rd, Līhuʻe
245-2145

Menehune Gardens
off Nāwiliwili Rd, north of harbor,
Līhuʻe 245-2660

Native Hawaiian Museum
Ching Young Village, Hanalei
826-7222

**Native Hawaiian Trading and Cul-
tural Center**
Ching Young Village

Old Koloa Town
Kōloa Rd

ʻOlu Pua Botanical Gardens
off Kaumualiʻi Hwy, Kalāheo
332-8182

Pacific Tropical Botanical Garden
Hailima Rd, Lāwaʻi 332-7361

Salt Ponds
between Port Allen Airport and
Salt Pond Beach Park, Hanapēpē
(Park 335-3551)

Smith's Tropical Paradise
Marina State Park, Wailua
822-4654/9599

Waioli Mission Church
Kūhiō Hwy, Hanalei 826-6253

Waioli Mission House Museum
behind Waioli Mission Church
826-6447, 245-3202

RESTAURANTS

AMERICAN

Bali Hai
Hanalei Bay Resort, Princeville
826-6522

Barbecue Inn
2982 Kress St, Līhuʻe 245-2921

Beach House
Spouting Horn Rd, Poʻipū
742-7575

Beamreach
Pali Ke Kua, Princeville 826-9131

Brennecke's Beach Broiler
2100 Hoʻone Rd, Poʻipū 742-7588

The Bull Shed
796 Kūhiō Hwy, Kapaʻa 822-3791;
Harbor Village Shopping Ctr,
Līhuʻe 245-4551

Cafe Hanalei
Sheraton Princeville, Hanalei
826-9644

Eggbert's
4483 Rice St, Līhuʻe 245-6325

Inn on the Cliffs
Westin Kauai, Līhuʻe 245-5050

Kokee Lodge
Kōkeʻe State Park, Kekaha
335-6061

Kountry Kitchen
1485 Kūhiō Hwy, Kapaʻa 822-3511

JJ's Boiler Room
Coconut Plantation Marketplace,
Kapaʻa 822-4411

JJ's Broiler
2971 Halekō Rd, Līhuʻe 245-3841

Jacaranda Terrace
  Kauai Hilton, Waipouli 245-1955
Keoki's Paradise
  Kiahuna Shopping Village, Po'ipū
  742-7534
Koloa Fish & Chowder House
  Old Koloa Town 742-7377
Lagoon Dining Room
  Coco Palms Resort Hotel, Wailua
  822-4921
Ono Family Restaurant
  4-1292 Kūhiō Hwy, Kapa'a
  822-1710
Prince Bill's
  Westin Kauai, Līhu'e 245-5050
Shell House
  Kūhiō Hwy at Aku Rd, Hanalei
  826-7977

CHINESE

Club Jetty
  Nāwiliwili Harbor, Līhu'e
  245-4970
Hanamaulu Cafe and Tea Room
  Kūhiō Hwy, Hanamā'ulu 245-2511
Ho's Garden
  3016 'Umi St, Līhu'e 245-5255
Kauai Chop Suey
  Harbor Village Shopping Ctr,
  Līhu'e 245-8790

CONTINENTAL

Charo's Restaurant
  5-7132 Kūhiō Hwy, Hā'ena
  826-6422
Gaylord's
  Kilohana Plantation, Kaumuali'i
  Hwy, Puhi 245-9593
Hale Kapa
  Sheraton Princeville, Hanalei
  826-9644

The Masters
  Westin Kauai, Līhu'e 245-5050
Midori
  Kauai Hilton, Waipouli 245-1955
Nobles
  Sheraton Princeville, Hanalei
  826-9644
The Tamarind
  Waiohai Resort, Po'ipū 742-9511
Voyage Room
  Sheraton Coconut Beach, Kapa'a
  822-3455
Waiohai Terrace
  Waiohai Resort, Po'ipū 742-9511

ITALIAN 137

Casa di Amici
  Kong Lung Ctr, 2484 Keneke St,
  Kīlauea 828-1388
Casa Italiana
  2989 Halekō Rd, Līhu'e 245-9586
I'ulani Isle
  Princeville Shopping Ctr, Hanalei
  826-7680

JAPANESE

Atami
  4-901 Kūhiō Hwy, Wailua
  822-1642
Hamura Saimin
  2956 Kress St, Līhu'e 245-3271
Kiibo
  2991 'Umi St, Līhu'e 245-2650
Kintaro
  4-370 Kūhiō Hwy, Wailua
  822-3341
Sharon's Saimin
  4-129 Kūhiō Hwy, Kapa'a
  822-5140
Tempura Garden
  Westin Kauai, Līhu'e 245-5050

MEXICAN

Norberto's El Cafe
4-1373 Kūhiō Hwy, Kapa'a
822-3362
Rosita's
Kukui Grove Ctr, Līhu'e 245-8561
Tropical Taco
Kapaa Shopping Ctr, Kūhiō Hwy,
Kapa'a 822-3622

SEAFOOD

Dolphin
Kūhiō Hwy near Hanalei River
Bridge, Hanalei 826-6113
Plantation Gardens
Kiahuna Plantation Resort, Po'ipū
742-1695

MISCELLANEOUS

Green Garden
13749 Kaumuali'i Hwy, Hanapēpē
335-5422
Makai
4-1421 Kūhiō Hwy, Kapa'a
822-3955
The Outrigger Room
Sheraton-Kauai, Po'ipū 742-1661
**Tahiti Nui Cocktail Lounge and
Restaurant**
Kūhiō Hwy, Hanalei 826-6277

BAKERIES

Crumb's Bakery
Kīlauea 828-1990
Green Garden
13749 Kaumuali'i Hwy, Hanapēpē
335-5422

Jacques
Oka St, Kīlauea 828-1393/1530
Kauai Kitchens
Kapaa Shopping Ctr 822-9992;
Rice Shopping Ctr, Līhu'e
245-4513 (and other locations)
Kauai Kookie Kompany
1-3959 Kaumuali'i Hwy, Hana-
pēpē 335-3291
Omoide
1-3543 Kaumuali'i Hwy,
Hanapēpē 335-5291
Popo's Cookies
Kūhiō Hwy, Waipouli 822-1573
Sweet Temptations
Princeville Shopping Ctr, Hanalei
826-9004
Tip Top Bakery
3173 'Akāhi, Līhu'e 245-2333
The Village Snack & Bakery Shop
Ching Young Village, Hanalei
826-6841

SWEETS

Banana Joe's Fruit Stand
Kūhiō Hwy near Kalihiwai on the
North Shore 828-1092
Lappert's Ice Cream Parlor
1-3555 Kaumuali'i Hwy,
Hanapēpē 335-6121
(and other locations)
The Nut Cracker Sweet
Coconut Plantation Marketplace,
Kapa'a 822-4811
Yogurt Patio
Waipouli Town Ctr, Kapa'a
822-0567; Kukui Grove Ctr, Līhu'e
245-7066
Zack's Famous Frozen Yogurt
Kiahuna Shopping Village, Kōloa
742-9769; 3-3257 Kūhiō Hwy,
Līhu'e 245-5269

FAST FOODS

Brick Oven Pizza
2488-A Kaumuali'i Hwy, Kalāheo
332-8561; Kukui Grove Ctr
245-1895
Dairy Queen
4302 Rice St, Līhu'e 245-2141;
Eleele Shopping Ctr, 'Ele'ele
335-5293; Kaumuali'i Hwy, Waimea
338-1911
McDonald's
3-3113 Kūhiō Hwy, Līhu'e
245-6123; 4-0771 Kūhiō Hwy,
Kapa'a 822-7290

Mustard's Last Stand
Lāwa'i
Pizza Hut
3-3171 Kūhiō Hwy, Līhu'e
245-9532; Waipouli Town Center,
Kapa'a 822-7433
Waipouli Delicatessen and Restaurant
Waipouli Town Plaza, Kūhiō
Hwy, Waipouli 822-9311
Wendy's
3160 Kūhiō Hwy, Līhu'e 245-9688
Zippy's
4-919 Kūhiō Hwy, Līhu'e
822-9866

SHOPPING

CENTERS

Ching Young Village
5-5190 Kūhiō Hwy, Hanalei
826-7222
Kiahuna Shopping Village
2360 Kiahuna Plantation Dr., Po'ipū
742-9562
Kilohana
3-2087 Kaumuali'i Hwy, Puhi
245-5608/7818
Kinipopo Shopping Village
Kūhiō Hwy, Kapa'a
Kukui Grove Center
Kaumuali'i Hwy, Līhu'e 245-7784
The Marketplace at Coconut Plantation (Coconut Plantation Marketplace)
484 Kūhiō Hwy, Kapa'a 822-3641
Princeville Center
5-4280 Kūhiō Hwy, Princeville
826-3320
Rice Shopping Center
4303 Rice St, Līhu'e 245-2033
Waipouli Plaza
Kūhiō Hwy, Waipouli

SHOPS

Ambrose's Kapuna Natural Foods
766 Kūhiō Hwy, Waipouli 822-7112
Andrade & Company
Coconut Plantation Marketplace
822-5821; Sheraton Princeville,
Hanalei 826-6321; Sheraton-Kauai,
Po'ipū 742-7388
The Art Shop
3196 'Akāhi St, Līhu'e 245-3810
Artisans' Guild of Kauai
Ching Young Village 826-6441
Big Save
Kapa'a 822-4971; Līhu'e 245-4088
Business Is Blooming
Kiahuna Shopping Village 742-1575
Cane Field Clothing Company
Kilohana 245-5020
Coco Palms Florist
Coco Palms Resort, Wailua
822-3772
Collectibles & Fine Junque
9821 Kaumuali'i Hwy, Waimea
338-9855

Coral Grotto
Kukui Grove Ctr 245-6619; Coconut Plantation Marketplace 822-9301

Coral House of Kauai
Menehune Shopping Village, Līhu'e 245-8190

Cowrie Shop
Coco Palms Resort, Wailua 822-7677

Crazy Shirts
Coconut Plantation Marketplace 822-3101; Kiahuna Shopping Village 742-9000; Old Koloa Town 742-7161

A Crystal Journey
Kilohana 245-3539, 800 521-63333

Da Latest Kine
Kaumuali'i Hwy, Waimea 338-1816

Farm Fresh Fruit Stand
4-1345 Kūhiō Hwy, Kapa'a 822-1154

Floratica Hawaii
PO Box 631, Kīlauea 828-1993

Flowers Forever
4444 Rice St, Līhu'e 245-4717; Princeville Ctr 826-7420

Flowers of the Rainbow
Pono Market, 4-1300 Kūhiō Hwy, Kapa'a 822-4781

Foodland
Princeville 826-9880; Waipouli Town Ctr 822-7271; Lihue Shopping Ctr, junction of Kūhiō and Kaumuali'i Hwys 245-6571

Gem
Lihue Shopping Ctr, junction of Kūhiō and Kaumuali'i Hwys 245-7067 (Record)

General Nutrition Center
Kukui Grove Ctr 245-6657

The Goldsmith's Gallery
Kinipopo Shopping Village 822-4653

HPI Pharmacy
3420 Kūhiō Hwy, Līhu'e 245-2471

Hale O' Health
Rice Shopping Ctr 245-9053

Half Moon Trading Co.
Kilohana 245-4100

Hanalei Camping & Backpacking
Ching Young Village 826-6664

Hanalei Health & Natural Foods
Ching Young Village 826-6990

Happy Kauaian
Coconut Plantation Marketplace 822-5813; Sheraton Coconut Beach, Kapa'a 822-4014; Sheraton-Kauai, Po'ipū 742-1366; Wailua Marina, Wailua 822-5911

Happy Talk Books
Kuahale Ctr, 5-5144 Kūhiō Hwy, Ste 3A, Hanalei 826-9446

Hilo Hattie's
Coconut Plantation Marketplace 822-3112

Island Camera & Gift Shops
Sheraton Princeville, Hanalei 826-9525; Coco Palms Resort, Wailua 822-3883

The Island Heritage Collection
Old Koloa Town 742-7583; The Hee Fat Bldg, Kapa'a 822-2324

Jack Wada Electronics
2981 'Umi St, Līhu'e 245-3321

James Hoyle Gallery
3900 Hanapēpē Rd, Hanapēpē 335-3582

Jim Saylor Jewelers
1318 Kūhiō Hwy, Kapa'a 822-3591

Kahana Kii Gallery of Koloa
Old Koloa Town 742-1408

Kahn Galleries
4569 Kukui St, Kapa'a 822-5281; Sheraton Princeville, Hanalei 826-6631; Coconut Plantation Marketplace 822-4277

The Kapaia Stitchery
Kapaia near Līhu'e 245-2281

Kauai Bay Cargo Company
Ching Young Village 826-6997;
Kapa'a 822-0752
Kauai Hidden Treasures
next to the Post Office near Waimea
Canyon Rd, Kekaha 337-1680
Kauai Images
4-1298 Kūhiō Hwy, Kapa'a
822-1950
Kaua'i Museum
4428 Rice St, Līhu'e 245-6931
The Kauai Queen
4447 Pāpālina Rd, Kalāheo
332-7060
Kerrysma
1316 Kūhiō Hwy, Kapa'a 822-1747
Kilohana Galleries
Kilohana 245-9352
Kinipopo General Store Wailua
4-364 Kūhiō Hwy, Kapa'a 822-3630
Koloa Casuals & Ocean Sports
5402 Kōloa Rd, Kōloa 742-7381
Koloa Gallery
Sheraton-Kauai, Po'ipū 742-7118
Koloa Gold
Old Koloa Town 742-7207
Koloa Men
5330 Kōloa Rd, Kōloa 742-9295
Koloa Mill
5406 Kōloa Rd, Kōloa 742-7349
Kong Lung Co.
Lighthouse Rd and Keneki St,
Kīlauea 828-1822
Lee Sands
Hawaiian Trading Post, corner of
Kaumuali'i Hwy and Kōloa Rd,
Lāwa'i 332-7404
Liberty House
Coconut Plantation Marketplace
822-3491; Kukui Grove Ctr
245-7751; Waiohai Resort, Po'ipū
742-6191
Lighthouse Gallery
Lighthouse Rd behind Kong Lung,
Kīlauea 828-1828

Lihue Pharmacy
Nāwiliwili 245-9547
Lina's Fashions & Fabrics
Rice Shopping Ctr 245-7211
Linda's Creation
4254A Rice St, Līhu'e 245-8480
Longs Drug Store
Kukui Grove Ctr 245-7771
Marta's Boat
770 Kūhiō Hwy, Kapa'a 822-3926
Matsuura Store
Lāwa'i 332-8641
McInerny's
Coconut Plantation Marketplace
822-9373
Menehune Food Mart
Kīlauea 828-1771 ; Kalāheo
332-8027
Nature's Gallery
947 Kuhio Hwy, Kapa'a
822-3789
The Nut Cracker Sweet
Coconut Plantation Marketplace
822-4811
The Only Show in Town
1495 Kūhiō Hwy, Kapa'a 822-1442
Pay 'n Save
4100 Rice St, Līhu'e 245-8896 (Pre-
scription)
Pearly Shells
2360 Kiahuna Plantation Dr., Kōloa
742-1767
JC Penney
Kukui Grove Ctr 245-5966
Plantation Stitchery
Coconut Plantation Marketplace
822-3570
Pono Market
4-1300 Kūhiō Hwy, Kapa'a
822-4581
Port of Kauai
Coconut Plantation Marketplace
822-0144
Princeville Galleries
Princeville Ctr 826-9151

Princeville Plantation Store
Princeville Ctr 826-9292
Puhi Store
Kaumuali'i Hwy, Puhi 245-2081
Rainbow Books
Kukui Grove Ctr 245-3703
Rainbow Rags
Rice Shopping Ctr 245-7074
Reyn's
Coconut Plantation Marketplace
822-7800
Say It With Flowers
1543-B Kūhiō Hwy, Kapa'a
822-5544
Sears
Kukui Grove Ctr 245-3325
Sea Reflections
Kilohana Plantation 245-5210
See You in China
Kukui Grove Ctr 245-8474
7-Eleven Food Stores
Kapa'a 822-1755; Hanamā'ulu
245-2110; Līhu'e 245-9422
Shanora of Kauai
Ching Young Village 826-7353
Shells International
Coconut Plantation Marketplace
822-3781
The Ship Store Gallery
Kiahuna Shopping Village
742-7123
Shoreview Pharmacy
4-1177 Kūhiō Hwy, Ste 113, Kapa'a
822-1447
Spinning Dolphin Designs
Ching Young Village 826-7461
Star Market
Kukui Grove Ctr 245-7777

Stones Gallery
Kukui Grove Ctr 245-6653;
Kilohana 245-6684
Swim Inn
Old Koloa Town 742-1115
Tahiti Imports
Coconut Plantation Marketplace
822-9342 (and other locations)
That Tropical Feeling
3450 Po'ipū Rd, Kōloa 742-9433
Toucans
Princeville Ctr 826-7332; Kinipopo
Shopping Village 822-1588
Town Store
Hanapēpē 335-5252
Tutu's Hale Keiki
Coconut Plantation Marketplace
822-3381
Tutu's Kiddy Korner
Kilohana 245-6578
Vicky's Fabric Shop
4-1326 Kūhiō Hwy, Kapa'a
822-1746
Village Variety
Ching Young Village 826-6077
Wainiha General Store
'Ananalu St, Wainiha 826-6251
Waldenbooks
Kukui Grove Ctr 245-7162;
Coconut Plantation Marketplace
822-9362
Westside Pharmacy
1-3845 Kaumuali'i Hwy, Hanapēpē
335-5342
Woodtrends
Keālia near Kapa'a 822-1173
Woolworth
Kukui Grove Ctr 245-7702

HAWAIIAN WORDLIST

These words are likely to be seen or heard by anyone visiting these islands. Some may be seen without the markings that alter pronunciation (and meaning), as explained in the INTRODUCTION. In the pronunciation guides given here, typical English syllables which most closely approximate the Hawaiian vowel sounds are used; a precise rendition would require long and complex explanations. The *'okina* [glottal stop] has been retained to show where adjacent vowels should not slide from one to the other. The *kahakō* [macron] shows where they are especially joined, almost as English diphthongs; syllables with elongated vowels are written twice and linked with the same mark. Stress is indicated by capitalization.

a'ā [AH-'AH] a rough, crumbly type of lava
aikāne [aye-KAH-neh] friend
akamai [ah-kah-my-ee] smart, wise, on the ball
ali'i [ah-LEE-'ee] chief, nobility
aloha a nui loa [ah-LO-ha ah NOO-ee LO-ah] much love
auē, auwē [ah-oo-EH-EH] alas!, oh dear!, too bad!, goodness!
'awa [AH-vah] traditional Polynesian drink wrung from the roots of the pepper plant (kava)
hana hou [hah-nah HO-oo] encore, do it again
hanohano [hah-no-HAH-no] distinguished, magnificent
haole [HAH-oh-leh] originally foreigner; now Caucasian
hapa [HAH-pa] half, part
hapa-haole [HAH-pa HAH-oh-leh] half Caucasian
Hau'oli Makahiki Hou [ha-oo-'oh-lee mah-ka-hee-kee ho-oo] Hawaiian translation of Happy New Year (now used, but not a traditional greeting)
haupia [ha-oo-PEE-ah] coconut pudding
heiau [HEH-ee-ah-oo] ancient Hawaiian place of worship
hele [HEH-leh] go, walk around
holoholo [ho-lo-HO-lo] to visit about, make the rounds
holokū [ho-LO-koo] a fitted, ankle-length dress, sometimes with train
ho'olaule'a [ho-'oh-lah-oo-LAY-'ah] celebration
hui [HOO-ee] club, association
hukilau [HOO-kee-lah-oo] community net-fishing party
hula [HOO-lah] Hawaiian dance
huli [HOO-lee] turn over, turn around
humuhumunukunukuāpua'a [hoo-moo-hoo-moo-noo-koo-noo-koo-ah-poo-AH-'ah] Hawai'i's State Fish; a small triggerfish famous for its long name
iki [EE-kee] little (size)
imu [EE-moo] ground oven
imua [ee-MOO-ah] forward, onward
kāhili [kah-ah-HEE-lee] a royal feathered standard
kahuna [kah-HOO-nah] priest, expert
kai [KY-ee] sea, sea water
kālā [KAH-lah] money (literally dollar)
kama'āina [kah-mah-AYE-nah] native born, longtime Hawai'i resident, old established family

kanaka [kah-NAH-kah] originally 'man' or person; now a native Hawaiian

kāne [KAH-neh] boy, man, husband

kapa [KAH-pah] tapa cloth (made from mulberry bark)

kapakahi [kah-pah-KAH-hee] crooked, lopsided

kapu [KAH-poo] forbidden, sacred, taboo, keep out

kaukau [KAH-oo-kah-oo] food

keiki [KAY-kee] child

kiawe [kee-AH-vay] mesquite tree

kōkua [ko-KOO-ah] help, assistance, aid

kona [KO-nah] winds 'that blow against the trades', lee side of an island

kukui [koo-KOO-ee] candlenut tree

kumu [KOO-moo] teacher

lānai [lah-NY-ee] porch, terrace, veranda

lani [LAH-nee] heaven, heavenly, sky

lauhala [lah-oo-HAH-lah] leaf of the pandanus tree (for weaving)

laulau [LAH-oo-lah-oo] bundled food in ti leaves

lei [LAY-ee] garland of flowers, shells or feathers, wreath

liliko'i [lee-lee-KOH-ee] passion fruit

loa [LO-ah] long

lomi [LO-mee] rub, press, massage, type of raw salmon (usually lomilomi)

lua [LOO-ah] toilet, restroom

lū'au [LOO-'ah-oo] feast, party, taro leaf

mahalo [mah-HAH-loh] thank you

mahimahi [mah-hee-MAH-hee] dorado or dolphin fish

māhū [MAH-hoo] gay, homosexual

makai [mah-KY-ee] toward the sea

make [MAH-keh] dead

makule [mah-KOO-leh] elderly, old (of people)

malihini [mah-lee-HEE-nee] newcomer, visitor

malo [MAH-lo] man's loincloth

mauka [MAH-oo-ka] toward the mountains, inland

mauna [MAH-oo-nah] mountain

Mele Kalikimaka [meh-leh kah-lee-kee-MAH-ka] Merry Christmas

Menehune [meh-neh-HOO-neh] legendary race of dwarfs

moemoe [mo-eh-MO-eh] sleep

mu'umu'u [moo-'oo-moo-'oo] long or short loose-fitting dress

nui [NOO-ee] big

'ohana [oh-HAH-nah] family, extended family

'ōkole [oh-oh-KO-lay] buttocks, bottom, rear

'ōkole maluna [oh-oh-ko-lay-mah-LOO-nah] Hawaiian translation of 'bottoms up' (a bit crude)

'ono [OH-no] delicious

'ōpū [OH-OH-POO-OO] abdomen, stomach

pakalōlō [pah-kah-LO-lo] marijuana

Pākē [PAH-keh] Chinese

pali [PAH-lee] cliff, precipice; *the* Pali=the Nu'uanu Pali

paniolo [pah-nee-OH-lo] cowboy

pau [PA-oo] finished, done

pau hana [pa-oo HAH-nah] finish work

pāhoehoe [pah-ho-eh-HO-eh] type of lava with smooth or ropy surface

pīkake [pee-KAH-keh] jasmine flower, named after 'peacock'
poi [POY] pasty food made from pounded taro
puka [POO-kah] hole, door
pūpū [POO-poo] hors d'oeuvres (literally 'shells')
tūtū [TOO-TOO] grandmother, affectionate term for old people—relatives or friends—of grandparents' generation (According to the rules of language set down by the missionaries, there is no 't' in the Hawaiian language, but hardly anyone ever says kūkū.)
'uku [OO-koo] fleas, head lice
'ukulele [oo-koo-LAY-leh] small, stringed instrument from Portugal
wahine [va-HEE-neh, wah-HEE-neh] girl, woman, wife
wikiwiki [wee-kee-WEE-kee] fast, in a hurry, quickly

PIDGIN ENGLISH WORDLIST

The pronunciation of pidgin is self-evident, and its spelling is phonic rather than fixed. In most cases, the derivation is also obvious. The lilt that is peculiar to this local lingo cannot be adequately described; it must be heard. This list is given as a guide to listening only. Trying to speak pidgin involves the risk of inadvertently saying something offensive or insulting. Everyone who speaks pidgin also understands correctly spoken English.

an den? So? What next? What else? [and then]
any kine anything [any kind]
ass right you are correct [that's right]
bambucha big
bambula big
beef fight
blalah heavy set, Hawaiian man, may be looking for a fight
bradah friend [brother]
brah short for bradah
buggah guy, friend, pest
bumbye after awhile, [by and by]
bummahs too bad, disappointed expression [bummer]
cockaroach rip off, steal, confiscate
cool head main ting keep calm, relax
da the
da kine anything being discussed, used as either noun or verb when the speaker can't think of the right word
dat that
dem them, guys, folks
eh? you know, do you understand?; also used at the beginning of a statement
garans guaranteed, for sure
geevum go for it! [give them]
grind eat
grinds food

had it destroyed, wrecked
haaah? what? I didn't hear you
haolefied like a haole
hele on go, leave, 'with it', 'hip'
high mucka mucka arrogant, conceited, elite
ho! exclamation used before a strong statement
how you figga? how do you figure that, makes no sense
howzit hi, hello, how are you doing, what's happening [how is it]
junk lousy, terrible
kay den okay then, fine
li'dat like that, short cut for lengthy explanation
li'dis like this
humbug trouble, bother
make 'A' make a fool of yourself [make ass]
make house make yourself at home, act like you own the place
mama-san local Japanese equivalent of 'mom' at 'mom and pop' stores
Maui wowie potent marijuana (from Maui)
minors no big thing, minor
mo' more
mo' bettah better, good stuff
moke heavy set Hawaiian male, often looking for a fight
nah just kidding (often nah, nah, nah)
no can cannot, I can't do it
o' wot? (added on to most questions, usually when the speaker is fed up) [or what]
poi dog mutt, person made up of many ethnic mixtures
Popolo black, Negro
shahkbait white-skinned, pale [shark bait]
shaka all right, great, well done, perfect, okay, right on
sleepahs flip flops, thongs [slippers]
stink eye dirty look, evil eye
talk story rap, shoot the breeze, gossip
tanks eh? thank you
tita heavy set Hawaiian woman, may be looking for a fight [sister]
try used at beginning of a command
we go let's leave
yeah? added on to end of sentences
yeah yeah yeah yeah yes, all right, shut up

RECOMMENDED READING

T here are countless books detailing the many aspects of Hawaiian history and culture, both ancient and modern. It has been impossible to detail these fascinating areas in a guidebook small enough to be handy. We recommend the following:

Atlas of Hawaii, **by the Department of Geography, University of Hawai'i,** University of Hawai'i Press, 1983. This book provides text on Hawai'i's natural environment, culture and economy along with maps.

The Beaches of Kaua'i County, **by John R.K. Clark,** University of Hawai'i Press, (in preparation). A complete guide to all the beaches of Kaua'i County, with maps, photographs, descriptions of facilities, emergency aid, suitability for various water activities and legends and lore associated with each area.

Bird Life in Hawaii, **by Andrew J. Berger,** Island Heritage, 1987. The story of the bird life of Hawai'i, including exotic birds and species which have become rare and endangered, each illustrated in full color accompanied by text written by the world's leading authority on Hawaiian birds.

Entertaining Island Style, **by Lavonne Tollerud and Barbara Gray,** Island Heritage, 1987. Menu planning is made simple in this colorful book. From lu'aus and beach parties to elegant Hawaiian suppers, there are many creative ideas for entertaining.

Favorite Recipes from Hawaii, **by Lavonne Tollerud and Barbara Gray,** Island Heritage, 1987. A collection of Hawai'i's most popular recipes. It includes Hawaiian cocktails, hors d'oeuvres, soups, salads, breads, main dishes, condiments, rice and noodles, vegetables and desserts.

Flowers of Hawaii, **photography by Allan Seiden and Loye Gutherie,** Island Heritage, 1987. A beautifully photographed guide to Hawai'i's colorful flowers, such as hibiscus, orchids and lilies, and their origins.

A Guide to Hawaiian Marine Life, **by Les Matsuura,** Island Heritage, 1987. Written by a marine educator at the Waikīkī Aquarium, this guide highlights the marine life in Hawai'i through description and color photographs.

Hawaii, **by James Michener,** Random, 1959. A novel about Hawai'i from its geological birth to the present, by this renowned author.

Hawaii: A History, **by Ralph S. Kuykendall,** Prentice, 1961. A good and readable overall history of Hawai'i from the first Polynesian voyages to statehood.

Hawaii: The Aloha State, **by Allan Seiden,** Island Heritage, 1987. Visit exciting Waikīkī, colorful Lahaina, majestic Waimea Canyon, historic Kona—all the Hawaiian islands are brought to life in this beautifully photographed book.

Hawaiian Dictionary, **by Mary Kawena Pukui and Samuel H. Elbert,** University of Hawai'i Press, 1986. Hawaiian-English, English-Hawaiian dictionary, regarded as the definitive reference for Hawaiian vocabulary. It contains folklore, poetry and ethnology compiled by the leading authorities of Hawaiiana and Polynesian languages.

Hiking Kauai, **by Robert Smith**, Wilderness Press, 1983. This guidebook lists hiking trails on Kaua'i, all personally trod by the author, with descriptions of the route, highlights, rating of difficulty, driving instructions, distance and average hiking time.

Historic Koloa: A Guide, **by Friends of the Koloa Community**, Friends of the Koloa Community-School Library, 1985. Compiled by a group of volunteers who interviewed old-timers, and combed archival and library sources for interesting old photographs and details of community history, this book presents a fascinating glimpse of the history of this charming Kaua'i sugar town.

The Illustrated Atlas of Hawaii, **by Gavan Daws, O.A. Bushnell & Andrew Berger**, Island Heritage, 1987. Illustrations of the Hawaiian island chain, native plants, birds and fish by Joseph Feher with a concise history.

The Journal of Prince Alexander Liholiho, **Jacob Adler, ed.**, University of Hawai'i Press, 1967. Young Alexander Liholiho and his brother Lot visited the United States, England and France on a diplomatic mission with Dr Judd. This diary records the impressions of the future king.

Kaaawa: A Novel About Hawaii in the 1850s, **by Oswald Bushnell**, University of Hawai'i Press, 1972. An historical novel set on O'ahu about the missionary period.

Ka'ahumanu: Molder of Change, **by Jane Silverman**, Friends of the Judiciary History Center of Hawaii, 1987. A biography of the most powerful woman in Hawaiian history and the vast changes she wrought in the social and political life of the kingdom she ruled.

Kahuna La'au Lapa'au (The Practice of Hawaiian Herbal Medicine), **by June Gutmanis**, Island Heritage, 1987. Authoritative and definitive work on Hawaiian herbs and the secrets of Hawaiian herbal medicine with colorful illustrations.

Kalakaua: Hawaii's Last King, **by Kristin Zambucka**, Mana Publishing Co. and Marvin/Richard Enterprises, Inc., 1983. This pictorial biography with more than 180 old photographs recounts the colorful reign of Hawai'i's last king.

Kauai, **by Bob Krauss**, Island Heritage, 1985. This stunningly photographed book, by Bill Gleasner, tells "The Story of an Island" rich in history and natural beauty.

Kauai, **by Allan Seiden, Island Heritage**, 1986. Seiden's photographs of beaches and sightseeing spots come alive in this brief overview of 'the Garden Isle'.

Kauai: A Many Splendored Island, **by Ronn Ronck**, Mutual Publishing, 1985. This large format book presents splendid photographs by Douglas Peebles showing the many faces of Kaua'i, in many moods. The text provides details and descriptions of the scenes, and provides glimpses of island history.

The Kauai Album, by Carol Wilcox, Kauai Historical Society, 1981. Enriched with many old photographs, this survey tells a lot about the island's European history, tracing the growth from villages of seven of Kaua'i's present towns, and presenting details of more than a hundred of Kaua'i's historically significant buildings.

Kauai: The Garden Isle, by Allan Seiden, Island Heritage, 1986. This colorful pictorial work explores the magic and beauty of the island including how it was formed, history and breathtaking views of different areas.

Na Pule Kahiko: Ancient Hawaiian Prayers, by June Gutmanis, Editions Limited, 1983. This collection of traditional Hawaiian prayers, in both Hawaiian and English, is annotated with fascinating detail about the contexts in which these prayers, and prayers in general, were used in the lives of ancient Hawaiians.

Niihau Shell Leis, by Linda Paik Moriarty, University of Hawai'i Press, 1986. An expert documentation of the traditions of this unique art, richly illustrated with color photographs of the many varieties of this rare and precious, gem-quality shell, and based on personal interviews with Ni'ihau women who are actively engaged in this ancient craft.

An Ocean in Mind, by Will Kyselka, University of Hawai'i Press, 1987. The extraordinary story of a 6000-mile trip from Hawai'i to Tahiti and back, the 1980 voyage of the *Hōkūle'a,* without the use of modern navigational aid. Navigator Nainoa Thompson, of Hawaiian descent, studied the stars, winds and currents to explore his Polynesian past.

Place Names of Hawaii, by Mary Kawena Pukui, Samuel H. Elbert & Esther T. Mookini, University of Hawai'i Press, 1974. Place names listed with pronunciation and translation where known. Includes names of valleys, streams, mountains, land sections, surfing areas, towns, villages and Honolulu streets and buildings.

Princess Kaiulani: The Last Hope of Hawaii's Monarchy, by Kristin Zambucka, Mana Publishing Co., 1982. Pictorial biography of Hawai'i's beautiful and tragic princess. Niece of Queen Lili'uokalani, Hawai'i's last reigning monarch, Princess Ka'iulani, was next in the line of succession to the throne.

Pua Nani, by Jeri Bostwick, photographs by Douglas Peebles, Mutual Publishing, 1987. Stunning color photography of the myriad blossoms—both native and introduced—that festoon these islands with their glorious hues and intricate structures.

The Return of Lono, by Oswald Bushnell, University of Hawai'i Press, 1971. A fictional reconstruction of the discovery of the Hawaiian Islands by Captain Cook.

Shoal of Time, by Gavan Daws, University of Hawai'i Press, 1974. An excellent and authoritative history of Hawai'i from earliest times to statehood, 1959.

Tropical Drinks and Pupus from Hawaii, by Lavonne Tollerud and Barbara Gray, Island Heritage, 1987. Delicious island cocktails and fruit drinks are complimented with a wide range of Hawaiian style hors d'oeuvres.

The Wilcox Quilts in Hawaii, **by Robert J. Schleck,** Grove Farm Homestead & Waioli Mission House, 1987. This lovely book not only presents beautiful color photographs of the entire collection of quilts held by Grove Farm Homestead Museum, it documents the lives of the missionary family who collected them and gives brief biographies of some of the local quiltmakers whose works are represented in this exceptionally well-preserved collection.

INDEX

APPENDIX

152

PHOTO CREDITS

1 Monte Costa
3 Scott Rutherford
5 Scott Rutherford
6 Scott Rutherford
7 Scott Rutherford
10 David Cornwell
11 Scott Rutherford
12 Scott Rutherford
14 Bob Abraham
15 David Cornwell
17 David Cornwell
18 Scott Rutherford
21 Scott Rutherford
23 Scott Rutherford
25 Bob Abraham
27 Bob Abraham
29 David Cornwell
31 Scott Rutherford
32 David Cornwell
33 Scott Rutherford
34 Scott Rutherford
35 Scott Rutherford
36 Scott Rutherford
37 Scott Rutherford
38 David Cornwell
39 Scott Rutherford
41 Scott Rutherford
42 Cyndi Parker
45 Scott Rutherford
46 Scott Rutherford
47 David Cornwell
48 David Cornwell
49 Scott Rutherford
51 Scott Rutherford
53 Scott Rutherford
54 Scott Rutherford
56 Scott Rutherford
59 Scott Rutherford
63 Scott Rutherford
65 Bob Abraham
67 Bob Abraham
68 Scott Rutherford
71 Scott Rutherford
73 Scott Rutherford
75 David Cornwell
78 Scott Rutherford
81 Ruth Gurnani-Smith
83 Bob Abraham
93 J. Carini
103 Scott Rutherford
115 Westin Kauai
116 Westin Kauai
120 Scott Rutherford
125 Scott Rutherford
127 Scott Rutherford
129 Scott Rutherford
130 Scott Rutherford
133 Scott Rutherford
135 Island Heritage

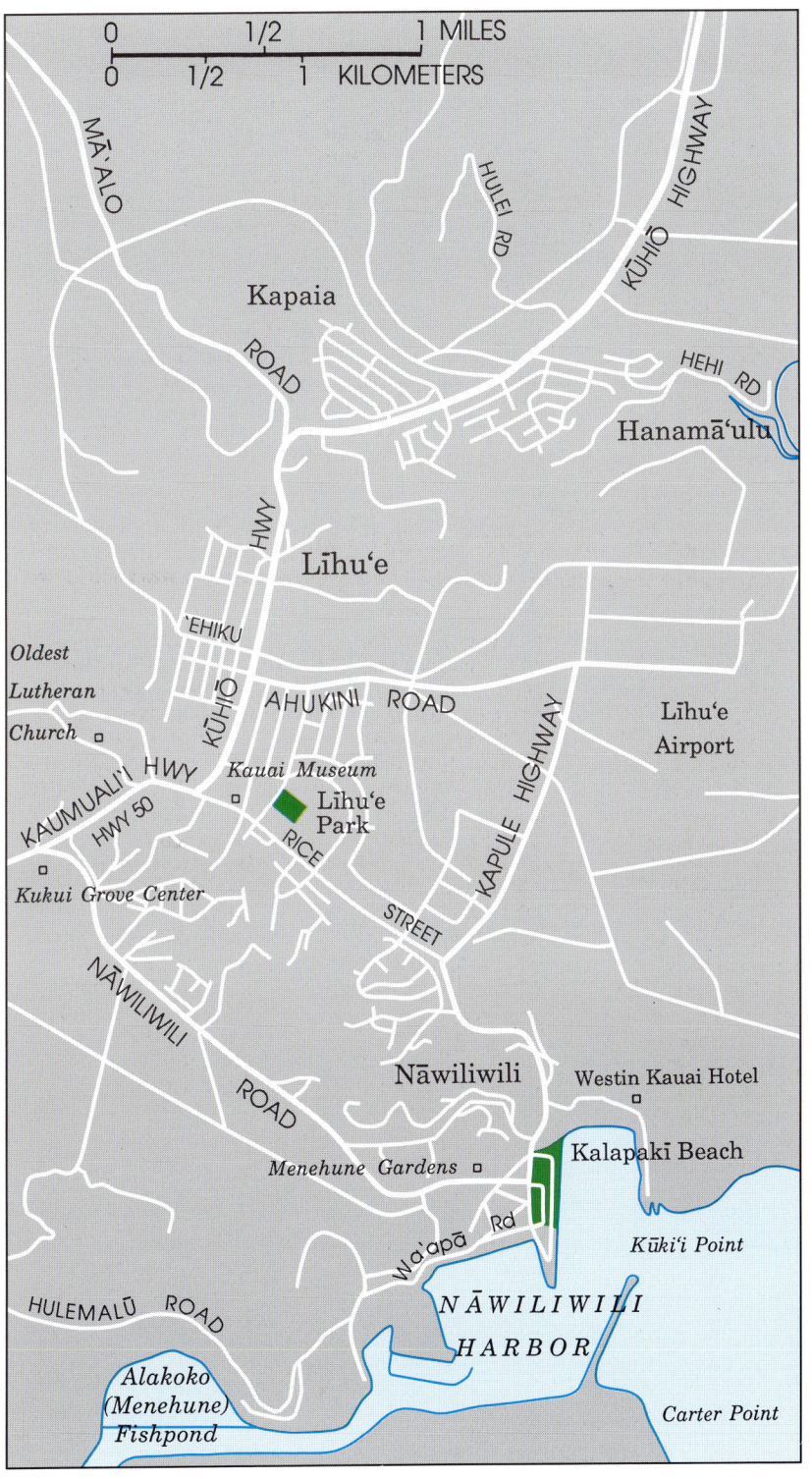

0   1/2   1 MILES

0   1/2   1 KILOMETERS

MĀʻALO

HULEI RD

KŪHIŌ HIGHWAY

Kapaia

ROAD

HEHI RD

Hanamāʻulu

Līhuʻe

HWY

Oldest
Lutheran
Church

ʻEHIKU

KŪHIŌ

AHUKINI ROAD

Līhuʻe
Airport

KAUMUALIʻI HWY

HWY 50

Kauai Museum

KAPULE HIGHWAY

Līhuʻe
Park

RICE

Kukui Grove Center

STREET

NĀWILIWILI

ROAD

Nāwiliwili

Westin Kauai Hotel

Kalapakī Beach

Menehune Gardens

Kūkiʻi Point

Waʻapā Rd

HULEMALŪ ROAD

NĀWILIWILI
HARBOR

Alakoko
(Menehune)
Fishpond

Carter Point

MALUHIA

ROAD

HWY 520

Waitā
Reservoir

ʻŌMAʻO

HWY

KŌLOA ROAD

RD

530

Old
Koloa
Town

Kōloa Park

WELIWELI   ROAD

private

private

private

Kōloa Mill

POʻIPŪ   RD

private

private

Kūhiō Park
Kahoai

HOʻONANI   ROAD

**Keawaloa
Bay**

Sheraton-Kauai Hotel

The Waiohai Resort

Poʻipū Beach Park

Kiahuna Plantation

Poʻipū

Makahūʻena Point

| 0 | 1/2 | 1 MILES |
| 0 | 1/2 | 1 KILOMETERS |